EYES, HANDS, BODY POSITION, AND RUN

Like H-E-Double Hockey Sticks

EYES, HANDS, BODY POSITION, AND RUN

Like H-E-Double Hockey Sticks

For the Ones Who Were Never Meant to Sit Still—
and Who Know It's Time to Build Something That Lasts

Clay J. Abernathy

ABERNATHY
PUBLISHING

Cover design by Clay J. Abernathy
Interior print design and layout by Marny K. Parkin
Ebook design and layout by Marny K. Parkin

Published by Abernathy Publishing

Paperback: 979-8-9941568-0-3
Ebook: 979-8-9941568-1-0

To the ones who were never meant to sit still.
To the builders, the fighters, the late bloomers,
and the ones who kept going even when no one was cheering.

And to my wife, Candice, and our five incredible kids—
Lyza, Lily, Jesse, Rose, and Dacey:
you're the reason I build anything at all.

Contents

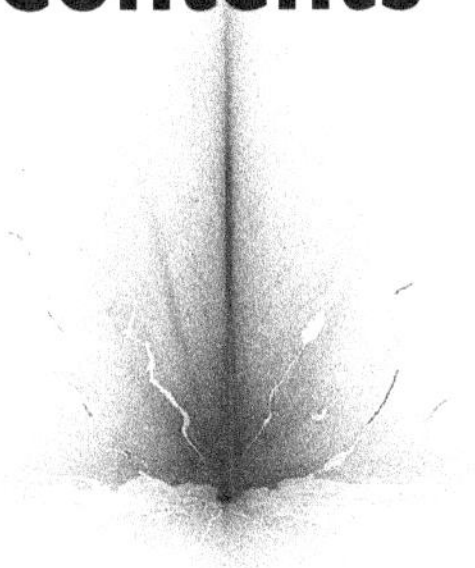

Why This Book, and Why Now

I shouldn't have made it. Statistically, I shouldn't even be here. But here we are. This is not a typical business book. It's also not just a memoir. It's both.

It's the real-life, messy, funny, sometimes heart-wrenching journey of a kid from Tucson who didn't come from money, didn't come from connections, and definitely didn't come from privilege—but found a way.

A way to build businesses. A way to build people. A way to build a life.

If you came looking for color-coded charts and buzzwords like *synergy* and *vertical integration,* you might be in the right aisle—but you've stumbled into something better.

If you've ever wondered whether you have what it takes to start something . . . if you've ever felt like your dreams were bigger than your resources . . . if you've ever hit a wall so hard you thought, *That's it; I'm done*—and still felt something in you whisper, *Not yet . . .*

Then you're exactly who this book is for.

What You're Going to Get

This is a collection of the stories that shaped me—professionally and personally. It's the greatest hits and biggest gut punches from my real life, told through the lens of someone who's lived in the grind and come out the other side with scars, stories, and a few wins.

Some chapters will make you laugh. Some might shake you up. And some will sneak up on you—right when you needed them.

You'll get lessons from working in sales and real estate, starting companies, building trade schools, and chasing big dreams with barely a budget.

You'll also hear about heartbreak, failure, insecurity, faith, family, and finding a reason to get back up again.

This book won't teach you how to build a business plan. But it might help you become the kind of person who can build *anything*.

The Blend

I don't separate life and business. Because I've never lived that way.

My faith affects my finances. My family affects my fire. And my failures? They've taught me more than any course ever could.

So yes—this is a business book. But it's also a love story. A comeback story. A "don't quit yet" kind of story.

Moments where I had to learn when to run, when to trust, and when to let go.

One Last Thing

I didn't write this book because I have all the answers. I wrote it because I've lived the questions.

I've stood in empty bank accounts. I've made payroll without knowing how. I've chased dreams so big they made people uncomfortable—and failed in front of them. I've hit walls that should have stopped me.

But they didn't.

Because somewhere inside, there was still something burning. A whisper: *There's more.* Not because I was special. Because I refused to stay stuck.

I wrote this book because I believe in people like you. People who've built something—or are still figuring it out. People who've failed, succeeded, compared, burned out, bounced back. Whether you're just getting started or already in the game, there's always another level. You don't need to be perfect. You don't need a mentor or a spreadsheet. You just need to keep moving.

And maybe you just needed someone to remind you—you're not behind. You're not alone. And you're definitely not done.

It's not theory. It's not fluff. It's lived experience from someone who's still in the fight, who's still building, who still believes the best things are ahead.

So if you're waiting for a sign . . . if you're hoping the clouds will part and the perfect moment will appear . . .

Let me be real with you: **It won't.**

There is no perfect moment. There is no golden door. There's just right now—and what you choose to do with it.

So breathe. Stand up. Square your shoulders. You don't need to have it all figured out.

You just need to take the next step.

What You'll Walk Away With

When you finish this book, you won't just have a list of lessons—you'll have something more dangerous.

You'll have the mindset to build when you have nothing.

The grit to keep going when everything says you should quit.

And the clarity to trust yourself when no one else does.

You'll walk away knowing:

- You don't need permission.

- You don't need perfect timing.

- You don't even need to have it all figured out.

You just need enough courage to move while everyone else is waiting.

And once you know that?

You're unstoppable.

Real Quick—Before We Take Off

This book doesn't read like a "normal" book.

Because I don't read like a normal human.

Honestly? I get bored halfway through most books.

I skim. I reread the same line six times. I think about tacos.

So if you're the kind of person who reads three pages, zones out, checks your phone, and somehow ends up reorganizing your sock drawer . . .

Congratulations. You're my people.

I wrote this book for us.

So when I wrote this, I didn't try to sound like an author.

I wrote it like a guy with ADD who just wanted to stay awake long enough to finish his own story.

That's why you'll notice a few things:

- **Some lines are bolded**—not to yell at you, but to help your eyes land where they need to.

- **Sections are short**—so you can burn through pages fast and feel like you're actually getting somewhere.

- The tone flips—**funny to serious to spiritual and back again**—because that's how real life happens.

- I break the rules. I repeat myself sometimes. I wander. And it all somehow works.

If you're the kind of person who struggles to finish books?
This one's for you.
If you're someone who reads three chapters, skips to the end, then decides if it's worth going back?
Also for you.
But if you've got a dream, a scar, a little fight in your soul, and a need to know that someone out there *gets it*—
Keep reading.
Because this story was written for the doers.
The builders.
The ones with big callings and messy starts.
The ones trying to fly without a runway
And if that's you?
Welcome to the book I never planned to write.

Introduction

I started hang gliding when I was twenty-two, and Shane was barely eighteen when he took his first flight right alongside me.

We learned together on the same bunny hills—both of us running (or, let's be real, fighting for our lives) down tiny slopes, just hoping to stay in the air long enough to feel like real pilots.

Dozens of flights, dozens of trips—watching each other improve, measuring airtime like it was a competition neither of us wanted to lose.

We'd razz each other over whose flight actually lasted longer, neither one willing to admit the other might have him beat.

Shane's father, Orrin Smith, was a legend.

The kind of guy who could ride thermals like he had a personal deal with the wind. At fifty-something, Orrin was outrunning us without breaking a sweat. He had been at this for decades, and his passion for flying was contagious. He passed that love down to Shane—and Shane passed it to me.

Shane wasn't just my flying buddy.

He was the kind of guy who made everything feel a little more electric.

Tall, athletic, and always grinning like he was in on a joke the rest of us hadn't heard yet, Shane brought energy into every space he entered.

Whether he was throwing on a kilt to impress the ladies or tossing a jacket over his shoulder like he was posing for a magazine cover, he didn't try to be cool—he just was.

He had this rare blend of confidence and humility.

He'd trash-talk your takeoff run, then spend fifteen minutes helping you put your wing away without ever needing the credit.

He loved flying—not just the rush of it, but the feeling of freedom. And he carried that same spirit off the hill, too.

He was the guy who'd drive hours just to hang out or send you a text midweek that was half ridiculous, half exactly what you needed to hear. He was your All-American kinda guy.

Learning to Fly

We started small. A grassy hill in Sonoita, Arizona. Not a mountain. Not even much of a hill, really—more like a suggestion of elevation. The kind of place where, if you tripped, you'd just stumble a little and end up with grass stains. But strap a glider to your back? Suddenly, that tiny hill looked like a launch pad to either glory or disaster.

In the beginning, just holding the glider was half the battle. It was bigger than us, heavier than we expected, and had a mind of its own.

The moment we tried to run, it would tilt to one side, and—**boink**—one of the wings would smack the ground, yanking us off-balance like a drunk trying to jog.

As we got a little stronger, we became reverse bobbleheads—our heads steady, but our bodies bouncing under the awkward weight of the glider as we fought to keep it level.

Then, after enough face-plants and frustration, we started to get the hang of it.

First, we'd skip—our feet barely leaving the ground for a half second, just enough to feel that tiny lift before gravity yanked us back down.

Then, after a few more hard runs and a little more confidence, it finally happened:

Flight.

It wasn't high.

It wasn't long.

But for the first time, we weren't just running with a glider—we were flying one.

Our instructor, Eric, drilled four things into us:

- **Eyes**—"Look where you want to go. You fly where you look." It's amazing how many pilots crash into trees while staring at them.

- **Hands**—"Tight on the ground, loose in the air." On the ground, you grip onto that glider. The moment you're airborne, you loosen up. Hold on too tight, and you'll fight the wing instead of letting it do what it was built to do. There's a time to control and a time to trust your wing.

- **Body Position**—"Different rules on the ground and in the air." On the ground, it's all about power and posture—shoulders square, chest forward, chin up, running tall like you mean it. You're the engine on takeoff, and if your stance is off, you're dragging the glider instead of launching it.

In the air, though? Relaxed, aligned, centered.

You fly with your whole body—shifting your weight, adjusting subtly. If your legs are flailing or your chest is out too far, you're working against the wing. Your body becomes the steering system, and small changes make a big difference.

- **Run Like Hell**—"If you don't run fast enough, you don't fly. You roll." And trust me, I watched plenty of bigger guys try—and fail—to hit takeoff speed. Doesn't matter how perfect your setup is—if you hesitate when it's time to commit, you're eating dirt.

It wasn't just about flying . . . It was about how to fly right. I didn't know it then, but those lessons would end up guiding me far beyond the sky. They shaped how I lead, how I build, and how I live.

The Quiet of Flight

The thing nobody tells you about flying a hang glider is how quiet it is. The moment your feet leave the ground, everything else just . . . falls away. The air is soft and steady, wrapping around you like an invisible current, quietly carrying you forward. It's just you and the wing.

If you turn hard enough, you can hear the wing slice the air—a sharp zip, like someone yanking a zipper open at high speed. It's the only real sound up there, that and the faint rush of the wind against your face.

You don't just move through the air—you feel it. You feel the pressure shift under your wing, the way the currents press against you, guiding you like an unseen hand. The air is alive beneath you, unpredictable and full of hidden power. A good pilot isn't just flying; he's listening—adjusting, reading every subtle cue the air gives him.

And in those moments, you're not just flying—you're a bird. Not in a metaphorical way. In a real way. No cockpit. No seatbelt. No machine keeping you aloft. Just you, your harness, and the wing on your back—trusting it completely to hold you in the sky.

It's not just thrilling . . . **It's romantic.**

Because it's just you up there, weightless, completely untethered from the world below. No emails. No phone calls. No deadlines. Just the feeling of floating, of existing in a way that people weren't really meant to, where the only thing keeping you from the ground is your own skill and the trust you place in your glider. And maybe that's why I loved it so much. Because when you're flying, there's no past, no future—just the sky.

The Thermal Rule

You can only fly to your next thermal.

A thermal is an invisible elevator made of warm rising air. The sun heats the ground unevenly—parking lots, rocky hills, and dry fields heat up faster than lakes or forests. That hot air rises, and if you're lucky enough to find it, it can lift you higher, sometimes thousands of feet. But here's the catch: You can't just fly forever, hoping another thermal will appear.

Every good pilot knows two things at all times:

1. Where the next thermal might be.

2. Where they're going to land if they don't find it.

Because eventually, you will run out of lift. And if you do and haven't been paying attention to your landing options, that's when things go bad—fast. You don't want to realize too late that you've drifted too far from a safe landing zone, with nothing but trees, power lines, or a Walmart parking lot below you. That was the game: Find lift, use it, move forward—but always be ready to land.

The Last Trip

A year into our flying days, Shane left for a two-year mission in Guatemala. And if you think hang gliding lit him up, you should've seen the photos from his mission—kids piled onto his shoulders, dirt roads stretching behind him, and that same big, mischievous grin—proof that it didn't matter where he was. Shane was always going to find a way to lift the people around him.

And when he came home?

He jumped right back in. Like no time had passed. Like the sky had just been holding its breath, waiting for him to come back.

That was Shane.

Effortless. Loyal. Full-send, all the time.

The kind of friend who made everything seem possible just by being next to you.

Some days, the wind didn't cooperate, so we'd go to the airport and get towed into the air instead. It wasn't the romantic kind of flying—not the effortless dance with the wind, not the weightless drifting where you feel like a bird. Tow launches were brute force.

The setup was simple: A long Kevlar cable stretched from your glider all the way to a pulley on the other end of the airfield, then back to a powerful motor designed to spool in the cable and yank you into the sky.

You'd clip in, take a deep breath, and give the signal.

Eyes, hands, body position, and run.

At first, it was slow—like getting towed behind a boat. But then, it kicked in hard. One second, you were rolling forward, the glider wobbling as it picked up speed, and the next—you were yanked straight into the air.

The force threw you back into your harness, the glider shooting upward at an aggressive angle—climbing fast, straight into the sky. It wasn't graceful. It wasn't natural. It was controlled chaos.

But then—at the top—you'd hit the release. The line would drop. The noise would fade. And for a moment, it was just you and the sky. That's how tow launches worked. Brute force up. Silence at the peak. Not beautiful—but effective.

And on this day? That was exactly the kind of flying we were doing. The air was dead still. No lift. No thermals. Just smooth, stable air.

Which meant no long, soaring flights—just quick up-and-downs, over and over.

And with fifteen of us out there, it actually worked out. Nobody was catching a thermal and hogging the sky for an hour.

We were all cycling through fast. Launch. Land. Go again. It wasn't a day for hero flights. But it was the kind of day where you could rack up launches—and we loved that.

Shane had brought his younger brother, Taylor, and a girl named Caitlyn—who was actually on her first date with him—to watch. The rest of us were taking turns flying, teasing each other about technique, and soaking in every second of the afternoon.

We were flying.

Burning through the daylight, one flight at a time.

And none of us—not a single one—wanted that afternoon to end.

We didn't know it yet, but everything we were learning about flying—about eyes forward, hands ready, running full speed into the unknown—was the same way you survive life.

As the sun started dipping behind the horizon, the flights slowed. It was almost time to pack up.

But we both wanted one more. I went first.

Eyes; hands; body position; run, baby, run!!!

I got in the air and detached the line, but something felt wrong and I heard yelling from below. I looked down and saw the line. It was still attached. I glanced down, and I was still dragging one hundred feet of tow rope. If that thing snagged on anything—a bush, a rock, even a stiff gust of wind—I'd be yanked straight into the ground like a cartoon character running off a cliff. But there wasn't anything I could do except pray it didn't catch before I landed.

Somehow, I made it back safely. As soon as I touched down, I felt an overwhelming sense of gratitude just to be on the ground. And then—man, I got an earful from Eric, our instructor. He wanted us safe, and he let me know exactly how reckless that situation had been. The crazy thing is, I was sure that I had released my line—I even felt the pop of the release. But to my surprise, it was still there. To this day, I still don't know what happened.

I stood there, staring at my glider, still trying to make sense of it. I had felt the release. I had done everything right. And yet, somehow, the line had still been there. I shook it off. At least I was on the ground. At least I had another launch and landing under my belt. And with the sun dropping lower, there was just enough time for one more.

Shane's turn.

We spliced the line back perfectly, checked every connection, and made sure everything was safe—every precaution, every step done exactly the same. The last thing we wanted was another mistake.

Then he looked over at me, grinning like nothing in the world could go wrong. I was still rattled from my own flight, still trying to shake off the feeling of barely making it down in one piece. But I didn't want him to see that. So I smirked back—just enough to sell it. Just enough to pretend I wasn't still thinking about the rope that nearly took me out.

He gave me a nod. I nodded back. No hesitation. No doubt.

"Eyes, hands, body position, run!"

And just like that, he was airborne.

We watched him climb. Smooth. Controlled. Just like every other flight that day. We saw the tiny blip of his release. He turned his hang glider back toward us and started flying in our direction. It was always best to land right back where you started so you didn't have to haul your glider back to the launch position.

As he started descending towards us from about three hundred feet, something went wrong. He was still attached to the line.

I screamed, "CUT THE ROPE!"

They did. But it was too late.

And then, it happened.

Fast. Brutal. Unforgiving.

One second, he was gliding, smooth and controlled. The next—his nose dropped hard. No hesitation. No recovery. Just a straight dive toward the ground.

For a split second, my brain refused to process it. Maybe it was the distance. Maybe it was my stupid optimism trying to convince me this was just another rough landing—something we'd laugh about later.

I told myself, *He'll pop up any second. He's fine. He's probably just shaken. Maybe pissed, but fine.* But he didn't pop up. He didn't move at all. I thought, *I better go check on him.*

When I got closer, I saw that he was completely wrapped up in his hang glider, tangled in the fabric and frame. Everyone was just standing around him, frozen, like they didn't know what to do.

For a second, it didn't feel real.

This was Shane—we had both taken our share of bad landings before. Any moment now, he was going to start untangling himself, maybe groaning about how annoying it was to get wrapped up like that.

But he didn't move. He was breathing. Barely. And I felt like standing there with them, but I quickly realized how alone he must have felt. So I dove in and held his hand.

I could feel it—his body fighting, his spirit wanting to stay, but his body giving up. Every breath was harder than the last. For a good thirty minutes, we talked through his breaths—me counting, him following.

"Breathe, Shane. Just one more. In . . . out. That's it."

I kept telling him, "They're coming. Just hold on. The paramedics will help you breathe when they get here."

And he did. Every single time, he listened. He fought.

But kneeling there, holding his hand, watching him struggle, I felt helpless. I had to do something. I had nothing to offer him but faith.

No medical training. No answers. Just faith. So I did the only thing I could think of—I gave him a blessing.

If you're not familiar with priesthood blessings, they're sacred in my faith. It's something we do when someone is sick, hurting, or scared. You place your hands on their head and speak—not just words, but *prayers led by the Spirit.* It's not magic. It's not theatrics. It's connection. Faith. Hope. Comfort.

And sometimes, if the Lord wills it—healing.

I knelt beside him, placed my hands on his head, and spoke. I didn't ask for a miracle. I didn't ask for time to rewind. I just asked for peace. For him. For us.

After the blessing, I told him, "You're not alone, Shane. Just keep breathing. Help is almost here." Then, finally—I heard it. A faint siren in the distance. I squeezed his hand. "They're almost here, Shane. Just hold on." And for a moment—he did.

I swear, as the sound grew louder, he relaxed just a little. Like he knew help was coming. Then the lights flashed into view. The paramedics rushed toward us, voices urgent, movements precise.

"Over here!" someone yelled.

The Final Effort

One of the paramedics leaned over him and gave a sharp command:

"Let's get him out of the glider."

We moved fast, carefully peeling the fabric and frame away from his body. The glider had wrapped around him like a cage, and every second mattered. We didn't lift—we braced, slid, and untangled.

Once he was free, we rolled him onto the spinal board. I moved with them, shifting to his head, cradling it gently, keeping his neck stable as they worked. I wasn't trained—but I was steady. And I knew he needed someone right there with him. I kept holding him, still counting in my head, still gripping the promise I had made:

They will help you breathe.

The first round of compressions started—hard, fast, mechanical. Another medic knelt beside us, prepping the bag valve mask and squeezing air into his lungs. But his chest still wasn't rising on its own.

They worked in sync—precise, focused, relentless. A team that had done this a hundred times before. Because they had.

Then, we heard it—the heavy rotor blades of a helicopter slicing through the sky. The flight medics had arrived. But then the helicopter touched down. And the flight crew? They moved like a different species. If the paramedics were pros, these guys were something else entirely. Faster. Sharper. Like they were plugged into a different frequency. No hesitation. No side talk. Just action.

They didn't waste a second. They moved with precision, purpose, urgency. This wasn't just protocol to them. As they took over, I still had a hold of his head, steadying him while we lifted him onto the stretcher. I climbed into the back of the ambulance, still holding his head in place, still feeling the weight of my promise. Inside, they worked fast. More hands. More equipment. More urgency. And now that there were four people working on him, they no longer needed my support.

I stepped out of the side of the ambulance—and my legs just gave out. I dropped to my knees on the hard dirt, my hands gripping the ground like it could somehow hold me together. And I prayed. Once again, I didn't beg for a miracle. I didn't ask for time to rewind. I just asked for peace. For him. For me. For all of us.

I could see it—they'd stopped working on him.

And as I forced myself up from the dirt, knees shaking, the ambulance doors opened. A paramedic stepped toward me, slow and heavy. He didn't have to say it. I already knew. The words were just a formality. My heart had already heard them.

"I'm sorry . . . He's gone."

I barely reacted. I had already made my peace with that part. But then, he kept talking.

"We're going to place him back on the ground."

And in the blink of an eye, I saw it. I saw Taylor, Shane's little brother, standing just a few feet away. I saw Caitlyn, the girl he'd brought on their first date, frozen in shock. I saw everyone who had gathered, waiting, hoping. And I knew—if they saw him being laid back on the ground, that would be the last image they ever had of Shane. That would be the moment burned into their memories forever.

No. Chance.

I blinked. My mind locked on to those words. I repeated them back to him.

"You're going to put him back on the ground? Right here?"

He nodded. "Yes."

I squared my shoulders, steadied my voice. "No. There is no chance that's happening."

The paramedic furrowed his brow. "We don't take dead bodies to the hospital."

I didn't even blink.

I took a slow step toward him so only he could hear me. "You're not pulling his body out of that ambulance and laying him on the ground in front of his little brother and a girl he just took on a first date."

I kept my voice low. Controlled. There were people gathered around. They didn't need to hear this. But he did.

He shifted uncomfortably. "I understand, but—"

I cut him off. "There aren't enough of you here to make that happen against me."

That landed.

I wasn't yelling. I wasn't pleading.

I was just stating a fact.

For a second, he didn't say anything. I could feel the weight of his hesitation, the battle happening behind his eyes. I let the silence sit. Let him feel it. Then I softened my voice—not because I was backing down, but because I needed him to understand.

"There's an easier way for this to happen."

I took a breath and leveled with him.

"You keep working on him. You fight with him until you get to the hospital. And then, you and I both get what we want."

Another pause.

He exhaled. Then, finally—he nodded.

And just like that, we were on our way.

The Call No One Should Have to Make

We made it to the hospital. They rushed him inside, and for a few seconds, I let myself hope. Maybe the machines could do what we couldn't. Maybe there was still time.

But it didn't take long.

A doctor stepped into the hallway, pulled me aside, and confirmed what I already knew.

Shane was gone.

After everything—the ambulance fight, the hospital, the doctors confirming what I already knew—there was still one last thing I had to do.

And in some ways, it was the hardest.

Because it wasn't about saving him anymore. It wasn't about holding his hand or keeping a promise. It was about *saying the words*. Words no father should ever have to hear from someone else.

Orrin was in Las Vegas for a chiropractor convention with his wife, and by now, they already knew something was wrong. Taylor had been keeping them updated—they knew he had crashed, they knew it was bad.

But no one had said it yet. No one had spoken the final words. That was my job. I pulled out my phone. Stared at the screen. It was my job to confirm it. I pressed call. And then—I couldn't speak. The second I heard Orrin's voice, the lump in my throat locked up my words. I tried to swallow, tried to force it down, but it felt like it took forever to get anything out. Finally, I managed to push out three words.

"Orrin . . . He's gone."

Silence. I could hear the noise in the background—life still happening while I sat in a hospital, saying the worst words I'd ever said.

Then finally, he spoke. I can't remember exactly what he said.

Grief messes with your memory. Everything felt foggy, heavy, unreal. But I do remember this: I asked him, "What do you want me to tell Taylor? How do you want me to break this to his little brother?"

And all he said was:

"Tell Taylor the truth."

That was it. No instruction. No breakdown. Just a father, handing me the weight he couldn't yet carry.

And just like that, it became my job to tell everyone.

One by one, as people arrived at the hospital, still clinging to some small hope, still believing for a miracle, I watched their eyes search mine—waiting for good news. And I had to take that away. I had to say the words that changed everything.

"He's gone."

I don't even know how many times I said it.

Again. And again. And again. Every time, I watched hope leave their faces. And that's when it hit me—this was my last job in all of this. I had fought to keep him alive. Now, I had to tell the world he was gone.

Falling Apart in the Next Call

I wasn't done. There was someone else I had to call. I pulled out my phone again and dialed. Candice. My wife. She was six days away from giving birth to our first child. I was supposed to be preparing for that, getting ready for the best moment of our lives.

Instead, I was sitting outside a hospital, telling her that Shane, someone she had personally grown up with, was dead. The second I heard her voice, I lost it. I bawled into the phone like a baby, like a kid who just wanted this all to be a mistake. I had held it together through everything—the crash, the paramedics, the hospital, the phone call to Orrin—but now, I just broke. I don't even know if I said words. I just cried.

And then, in the middle of my own sobbing, it hit me. This is my wife. We were about to walk into something we'd never faced before—and she didn't need me falling apart. She needed her husband at her side, locked in and ready to face it with her. Our daughter was days from arriving. There was no time to break down, no time to grieve.

And that's when I remembered my own rule—the one I made back in my Cutco days: **You get one minute.** One minute to fall apart, cry, be negative. But after that? Clock's up. Find the positive and move on.

I know that sounds ridiculous in a moment like this. But honestly? It worked.

Right there, on that phone call, I stopped crying. I wiped my face, steadied my breathing, and told Candice what had happened. Then I did the only thing I could do: I went home—not just to welcome a baby girl, but to become a father. To her. To the ones who would follow. To the life we were building.

Shane was gone. And I could've stayed stuck in that moment—frozen in grief, replaying every what-if. But life doesn't wait for you to heal. It moves forward; ready or not, here it comes.

The grief stayed, but I made room for something bigger: love, responsibility, and the sacred weight of showing up. And here's what I've learned—the brain is incredible. It will do what you tell it to do. If you tell it to find the good, it will start looking. That's exactly what I made it do.

You don't always get to control the outcome. But you do get to control whether you show up.

I want to enjoy every minute of my life. And I know if I stay stuck in one moment, I'll miss other great ones. It's good to reflect and replay the hard moments—to learn from them, to make sure you don't repeat the same mistakes. But the negative what-ifs? Those only hurt you. They keep you locked in the past when the best parts of your life are still waiting to be lived.

Chapter 1

The First Five Dollars

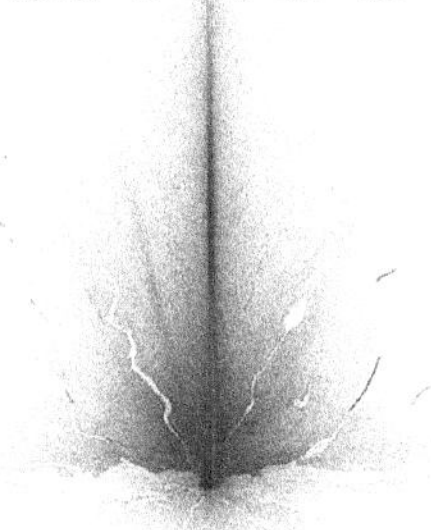

I grew up poor. And I don't mean the kind of poor where you didn't get the new Nikes. I mean food stamps that looked like Monopoly money, government cheese, and groceries from the church kind of poor. We had five kids in the house—Jesse, Mya, Scott, me, and Tania—and one more who wasn't with us. My brother Clint died at birth, but my parents never left him out. Anytime someone asked how many kids we had, they said six. That tells you a lot about who they were.

My parents came from pain. Both grew up in alcoholic homes—places full of yelling, silence, and survival. My dad lost both of his parents by sixteen. My mom's dad walked out and never really came back. Her mom was an alcoholic I met once, and once was plenty. So I didn't grow up with grandparents or generational warmth. But my parents had something more powerful: faith in Jesus Christ and a fierce commitment to do better. They worked like crazy—running a dance studio, scraping together side jobs—just trying to hold it all together. We didn't have money, but we had values. And noise. Lots of noise.

Each sibling played a role in that chaos. Jesse, ten years older than I, was the missionary-turned-married guy who always seemed like he had it together. Mya was the gentlest person I've ever known and practically raised me while my parents were working. Scott was the hands-on genius I idolized from a distance, even if he didn't want me tagging along. And Tania, my little sister, probably got the most tender version of me—when I wasn't too busy trying to impress my brothers. I was the tagalong, the one always trying to be included. My brothers protested every time my mom told them to bring me somewhere . . . but their friends didn't. Their friends would shut it down quick: "Nah, let him come." They treated me like I belonged. And in a loud house where compliments were rare and approval was hard to come by, that mattered more than they knew. We didn't hand out compliments in our house. If anything, insults were our love language. But deep down, we all wanted something more. We wanted more than we had. More than we got. And I think that hunger shaped us—for better or worse. It taught us to hustle, but it also taught us to hide. We loved the way we grew up, and we hated it at the same time. And somewhere in the middle of all that contradiction, I made a quiet decision: I was going to build something more—with my life, my words, and maybe one day, with my hands.

Grocery trips weren't casual—they were missions. And back then, food stamps weren't discreet. Not even close. They came in paper booklets filled with colorful bills—orange, blue, brown, green—like Monopoly money, but worse, because everyone in line knew exactly what they were. There was no quiet way to use them. You had to tear them out one by one at the register, each riiip echoing like a siren: "Hey everyone—we're broke!" My mom stood tall anyway. Me and my brother flanked her like bodyguards—heads on swivels, scanning the store, doing everything we could to help her move through that moment with dignity.

And if the stamps weren't enough of a spotlight, we also had the coupons. A stack of clippings, folded and sorted, like we were trying to game the system with scissors and prayer. Not just one or two coupons—dozens. Sometimes for ten cents off. Sometimes more. And every one of them had to be laid out, scanned, and verified while the line behind us grew and the stares got louder.

But the real stress came when we had to buy something that wasn't food. Like soap, hair products, or toilet paper. Those weren't covered by food stamps. So now, while my mom was tearing out rainbow bills and handing over a deck of coupons, we also had to pull together real cash—for the extras. And I don't mean crisp bills. I mean coins. Change from the ashtray. The bottom of her purse. A crumpled dollar or two, if we were lucky. Everything we had in that moment to get by.

And if someone familiar walked in while we were in line? Forget it. My mom would yank the cart out like we were making a getaway and loop back around the aisles to "grab something we forgot" until the coast was clear. We couldn't risk anyone seeing us pay with those food stamps. That was the rule.

And honestly? That whole survival mindset became part of my life. The strategy, the instincts, the constant pressure to read the room and adapt. That creativity and problem-solving? Yeah, that would come in real handy later—especially once the utilities started getting shut off and I was figuring out how to give girls the number to a grocery store pay phone. But we'll get to that.

For now, let's rewind to where it really started—when I was five years old and decided I needed a buzz cut.

One of the cool kids at school had one, and obviously, I needed to match the vibe. But it was five bucks for the haircut, and that wasn't exactly in the family budget. After some serious begging, my mom finally caved and paid for the first one. But she made it very clear: "This is a one-time thing. After this, you're paying for your own haircuts."

Challenge accepted.

Turns out, freshly buzzed hair is irresistible. My older siblings and their friends kept rubbing my head like I was a magic lamp. So

I did what any reasonable five-year-old would do—I started charging a quarter per head rub. No freebies. You want the magic? That'll be twenty-five cents.

And it worked. I grinded my way to five bucks and paid for my next haircut myself. Five years old, running my first business out of the living room.

And honestly? That was it. That was the moment I realized how life works. Find a way. Make it happen. Earn it.

That little grind planted a seed. It taught me that nobody's coming to save you. Nobody's handing you what you want. But if you're willing to get creative, put in the work, and charge a few quarters for head scratches, you might just get where you want to go.

It wasn't much, but that was the first time I figured out how to work for what I wanted.

And that's really where the grind began.

Chapter 2

The Beef Jerky Business

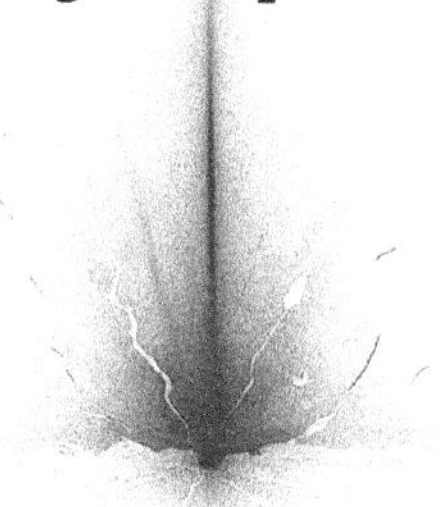

By sixth grade, I had already figured out that if you're good at something, people will pay you for it. But I didn't set out to start a business. Honestly, I was just trying to make something we couldn't afford.

See, beef jerky was way out of our price range growing up. That stuff was a luxury. Buying it at the store wasn't even a conversation. But then one of our neighbors gave us an old dehydrator. Probably thought we'd use it for apples or bananas or something healthy like that. Nope. I had bigger plans.

I thought, *Why don't I make jerky for us?*

My mom, being the MVP she always was, used a mix of food stamps and donated meat from the church to hook me up with the supplies. I started messing around with recipes—experimenting with flavors, slicing the meat just right, running batches through the dehydrator, adjusting the seasoning until I felt like I had it dialed in. Before long, I had made some seriously good jerky.

At first, it was just for the house. I figured if we couldn't afford jerky, well, I'd just make it. Problem solved.

Then one day, I brought some to school. Not to sell. Just as a snack. I shared a piece with a kid sitting next to me. He took one bite, looked at me, and said,

"Man . . . I'll buy that from you."

And just like that, my first sale.

The next day, I brought a little more. Same thing—gone. Word started getting around, and before I knew it, I was running a full-on jerky operation out of my backpack. Kids were skipping cafeteria food and throwing their lunch money at me.

The first time I brought a full batch, I sold out before lunch was even over. I came home with sixty bucks from about fifteen dollars' worth of supplies. I handed my mom the cash to cover what she'd spent, and just like that, we were in business.

For a little while, anyway.

Because there's always that kid. You know the one. The guy who thinks he's too good to pay.

One day, he comes up asking for a free piece. I tell him, "Nah, man. Everyone pays." Apparently, that wasn't the answer he wanted, because the next thing I know, I'm getting called to the principal's office.

Now listen, me and the principal? We had a relationship. By that point, I was practically on a subscription plan. I mean, we were on a first-name basis. I was usually in there because some poor teacher had tapped out after trying to contain my energy for an hour. I'd sit in that chair, he'd give me The Look, and then it was always the same thing:

"Clay, you've got three days of detention."

Clockwork.

But this time felt different.

Because this time, I wasn't there for talking too much or pushing the limits. I was there because I'd accidentally launched an underground jerky cartel right under his nose.

I walked in expecting the usual: stern face, quick punishment, back to class. But when I sat down and explained what happened, I watched it happen in real time—this man who had probably written me off as just another troublemaker actually cracked a smile.

The man who spent most of his career shutting me down . . . for the first time . . . genuinely looked at me like, *Well, I mean . . . That's kind of impressive.*

He shook his head and said, "Clay . . . You can't sell jerky at school. It's against the rules."

And I'm sitting there thinking, *Okay, but . . . Have you tried it?*

So naturally, I slid the bag across his desk, like we were making some backroom deal.

"Come on, just one piece. Just try it."

He looked at the bag. Paused for a second.

And then pushed it right back.

"No deal."

Business closed.

And honestly? Yeah, I was disappointed. I had a good thing going. But sitting in that chair, watching the man who normally handed out detentions like candy finally see me as more than a problem? I gotta admit . . . That was a win on its own.

And more importantly, by then I already knew the truth:

If you've got a skill, you've got a shot. Whether it was jerky, head scratches, or whatever came next—I was going to figure out how to make something happen.

The principal may not have appreciated it, but the grind was alive and well.

Chapter 3

Snappy the Clown

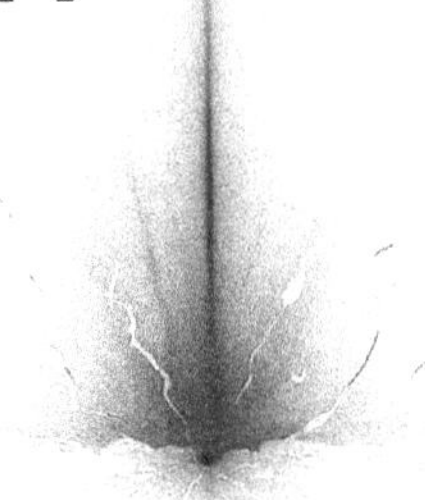

Somewhere between charging a quarter to rub my buzzed head and selling beef jerky out of my backpack, I stumbled into something a little . . . different.

Balloon animals.

It all started with a trip to Barnes & Noble—a place we had no business being. We couldn't afford books from there. We couldn't even afford books from the *library*. We had ruined so many over the years—lost covers, torn pages, water damage from who knows what—that our late fees were stacked up like a mortgage. Eventually, they cut us off. No more borrowing until we paid. And paying wasn't happening.

So I don't remember exactly why we were at Barnes & Noble that day—maybe killing time, maybe escaping the heat, maybe just pretending like we belonged in a world with lattes and laminated price tags. But there we were. And that's when I saw it.

A balloon animal kit.

It wasn't just a book—it came with balloons and a guide that showed you how to make everything from a basic dog to a full-on bear.

The pictures were bright, the instructions looked doable (kind of), and I was instantly obsessed. I held it in my hands like it was treasure.

My mom didn't see it that way.

"You're never going to do anything with that," she said, already heading down the aisle. But I couldn't let it go.

"Look," I told her, "I'll pay you back. I've got fifteen bucks at home."

Which may or may not have been true. But in that moment, I meant it. Somehow, I *would* pay her back.

And, surprisingly, she agreed.

She bought me the book.

That's just who she was. My parents didn't have much, but they would give everything they had if it made one of us happy. It's probably why we were always broke. My mom knew I didn't really have the fifteen bucks. But she also knew I'd figure it out—or maybe she just didn't care. I had been pulling weeds, knocking doors, doing whatever odd jobs I could. And yeah, I paid her back. But if I hadn't? She still would've done it. She would've given me her last dollar without blinking. Because to her, seeing her kids light up was worth more than money ever could be.

Anyway—back to the book.

It didn't come with a pump.

Nope. No easy shortcut. If you wanted a balloon dog, you were going to blow until either the balloon gave in—or your dignity did. It was a test of lung power, patience, and how much latex-related trauma one child could endure. But I was all in.

I took that book home like it was sacred. And I went to work. I made every single balloon animal in it. Every sword, every hat, every poodle. If it could be twisted, I twisted it. My room looked like a balloon zoo exploded. I burned through that first little bag of balloons so fast I couldn't believe it. And we couldn't exactly just run out and buy more supplies—balloons weren't in the budget.

That's when Terry and Kenny, our neighbors across the street, stepped in. They saw what I was up to and one day surprised me with a giant bag of balloons—hundreds of them. No birthday, no reason, no strings. Just kindness.

And you have to understand . . . This wasn't normal. People didn't just spend their own money helping some broke kid down the street with his goofy balloon hobby. But that's the kind of people they were. They believed in me before there was even anything to believe in.

And they weren't the only ones.

Chris Snodgrass, one of our other neighbors, noticed my balloon skills were leveling up fast. Most adults would've smiled politely and said, "That's cute, Clay," and moved on. But not Chris. She actually *paid attention.* She was a high school teacher, and one day at her school's job fair, a professional balloon artist and entertainer showed up looking for high school students to train—someone older, reliable, and ready to work.

Chris didn't hesitate. She said, "I know a kid—but he's . . . let's just say *not exactly* high school." I was barely out of elementary school, still figuring out how to keep my shoes tied—and suddenly, I was on my way to becoming a balloon artist's apprentice.

And honestly? This was a *huge* break. Up to that point, balloons were just something I thought was fun. But this guy saw it as a business. He showed me how to turn a hobby into real money—for both of us.

Before I knew it, I was learning his top-tier balloon tricks and figuring out how to handle real gigs. He even introduced me to a friend who had worked with the Ringling Brothers, and that's where I picked up the ins and outs of full clown makeup. The juggling? I figured that out on my own—with a little help from my dad.

I started out juggling whatever I could find around the house—mostly fruit from the kitchen. Oranges, apples . . . anything round enough to stay in the air for a few seconds. Once I started making real money from gigs, I reinvested back into my act and upgraded to proper juggling gear: bouncy balls, beanbags, rings. I even taught myself a few off-the-ground tricks. Nothing Cirque du Soleil level, but just enough to stand out—and enough to market myself as the full package: balloon artist, face painter, and juggler.

Little by little, it all came together:

- Balloon skills

- Juggling act

- Full clown makeover

And just like that, Snappy the Clown was born.

Purple wig. Full face paint. My dad's oversized suit with a pillow stuffed in the belly to give me that *classic* clown look. The whole thing.

My first big gig was the Spring Fling in Tucson, and man—I'll never forget it. I was twelve years old, and you'd think I'd be nervous. Nope. I was *pumped.* This was the big leagues. I was making fifty-five dollars an hour—and it was a two-hour job. That's one hundred and ten dollars cash for one afternoon of clowning around. You couldn't tell me *anything* after that. I walked out of there like I was the CEO of Clown Enterprises.

There I was, making balloon animals, juggling, running my clown routine—and the only weird part? Everyone kept calling me "ma'am." I hadn't exactly hit my growth spurt yet, and with the wig and makeup, I guess Snappy the Clown looked a little more like Snappy the Clownette. But honestly? I didn't care. I was too busy having the time of my life—and getting paid for it.

And after that? Business took off.

At first, it was a few gigs a month. But pretty soon, my schedule was packed: every Tuesday and Friday night, plus one to three parties every weekend. Birthday parties. Pizza Huts. School carnivals. You name it—I was there.

For years, that was my thing. All through high school, I made a living as a full-blown clown. And honestly? I loved it. It was fun, it paid great, and best of all—it kept me out of trouble.

Looking back, it's funny. Nobody dreams of growing up to be a clown. But man . . . That clown grind carried me for a long time.

None of it would've happened without a few true believers—people who looked at a scrawny kid with a balloon bag and thought, "Yep, that one's got circus lungs."

Chapter 4

If You Can't Play the Game, Get Paid to Watch It

I don't actually think I was a fast learner. Not naturally, anyway. While other kids picked things up fast, I was the one standing off to the side, trying to figure out *why* it worked and how all the pieces fit together. Being the fourth kid probably had a lot to do with that. I grew up watching my older siblings pull off stuff I wasn't allowed to do yet—and I wanted in. I didn't just want to keep up; I wanted to *beat them at their own game.* So even if it took me twice as long, I stuck with it until I cracked the code.

Whether it was selling beef jerky, twisting balloon animals, or charging kids a quarter to rub my buzzed head, I wasn't just playing around—I was building my mini empire, one weird hustle at a time.

And that mindset followed me everywhere.

At the same time the whole clown thing was taking off, I was also getting introduced to baseball—and, without realizing it, learning another business. Before ADD was a recognized thing, I was just a kid who wanted to do *everything.* Sports, business, whatever—I was in. My brain was like a pinball machine, bouncing between big dreams and bigger distractions.

Looking back, that was both a blessing and a curse. On one hand, I was constantly juggling way too much. On the other? I wanted to **understand it all**—and that kept me going. Whether it was baseball or balloons, I jumped in with both feet and took it seriously.

But when I was younger . . . I really wasn't *built* for sports.

Picture a human bobblehead—huge noggin, tiny little body, running around like I might tip over if I moved too fast. That was me. Baseball? Yeah, no. That wasn't happening. I wanted to be good. I tried. But every time I stepped up to the plate, I looked like I was swinging a sword on a pirate ship. My helmet would slide down over my eyes, I'd miss the ball by a mile, and I'd end up spinning in a circle like a cartoon.

Still, I *loved* being around the game. I loved the crowd. The energy. The rhythm of it. I just didn't have the coordination to actually play.

And that's when my buddy's dad—who was an umpire—threw me a lifeline.

"Hey, you can make ten bucks a game if you umpire."

That was it. No application. No tryout. Just a chance.

Ten dollars a game might not sound like much, but at eleven years old, it was a fortune. And more than that—it was a role. A uniform. A reason to show up and matter. My *big clown break* hadn't happened yet, and my beef jerky business had just been shut down (thanks a lot, school rules), so umpiring became my first real shot at making money the *legal* way. I traded my glove for an umpire's mask and got to work.

I wasn't just there for the paycheck. I wanted to *nail it*. I studied the rulebook, watched the older umpires, and soaked up everything I could. When someone finally trusted me with real responsibility, I made sure I *earned it*.

And from there, the work never really slowed down.

By high school, my schedule was slammed.

Classes all day. Wrestling practice right after. Clown gigs on Tuesdays and Fridays. Birthday parties every weekend. Little League umpiring in the spring. If it paid or gave me a shot at getting better at something—I was in.

I wasn't doing it because someone was pushing me. I was doing it because I wanted more. More than what I'd grown up with. More than what people expected from a kid like me. I didn't have the luxury of sitting still. If I wanted a different life, I had to earn it. Every hour, every dollar, every rep.

And if there was one thing that helped keep me sane through all of it—it was wrestling.

Wrestling didn't just teach me how to fight. It taught me how to suffer well. How to push through pain. How to perform under pressure. How to stay focused when your lungs are burning, your legs are shot, and the only thing keeping you moving is your willpower.

It didn't matter how tired I was from school, how many clown gigs I had coming up, or how many birthday parties were on the calendar—when I stepped on the mat, nothing else existed. It was just me and the grind.

And that grind? It sharpened me. It gave me a mental toughness that bled into everything else. Once you've spent two hours in a sweatbox of a gym, cutting weight, getting tossed around by guys who are stronger, faster, and meaner than you—man, juggling balloons or calling balls and strikes doesn't feel all that tough.

Wrestling taught me that your body has limits, but your mind decides whether you quit.

I kept that attitude with me as I moved on to bigger challenges. Including one of the first real jobs I ever had—construction. It wasn't glamorous. It wasn't easy. But it was real. Real work. Real sweat. Real money.

I started around sixteen, working for my buddy's dad during the summers in Tucson, Arizona—where it regularly hits a hundred and fifteen degrees and the shade feels like a rumor. You're not just sweating—you're melting. We'd be out there early, barely awake, swinging sledgehammers, loading debris, hauling buckets of tile, cutting lumber, running backhoes—whatever needed to be done. By noon, your shirt was stuck to your back, your hands were blistered, and the ground was hot enough to cook breakfast.

And the pay? Let's just say clown money was looking pretty good by comparison. I was still making more by twisting balloons into giraffes than I was by tearing out drywall. So no, I wasn't dreaming of a future in construction just yet. But I showed up. I worked. I learned.

And what I didn't realize at the time was that those long, blistering summers were planting seeds. Skills I didn't know I'd use. Experience I didn't know would matter. I thought I was just stacking odd jobs and paychecks. Turns out, I was stacking tools.

But even with that work ethic, even with the drive—I still thought I needed a *big* dream to chase. And I had one.

Plan A: Fighter Pilot for the Navy

Since I was a kid, I had one dream: fly fighter jets.

Fast jets. G-forces. That perfect mix of speed, danger, and control. I didn't just think it was cool—I *felt* it in my bones.

I devoured books on fighter pilots. Watched every documentary I could find. Studied flight patterns like it was a subject in school. And when *Top Gun* came on? Forget it. I was Maverick. Couch Cushion cockpit. Sunglasses inside. Fully locked in.

That wasn't just a fantasy—it was the plan.

I knew what I wanted, and I was willing to work for it.

Then, at fourteen years old—boom.

My heart started racing one day. Not the butterflies-from-talking-to-the-cute-girl-in-math-class kind of racing. I'm talking full-blown, out-of-control, can't-slow-it-down, what-the-heck-is-happening kind of fast. Like my chest was trying to beat me in a sprint.

Diagnosis: Supraventricular Tachycardia. SVT.

My heart had a wiring issue. A short circuit.

It would misfire and speed up like I was mid-dogfight—but I'd just be sitting on the couch.

Surgery was the only option.

And that's when everything shifted.

The procedure wasn't open-heart—ten years earlier, it would've been—but it was still intense. The plan was to thread wires up through my groin and neck, trigger the misfire, and burn off the faulty part. Sounds simple until you realize they keep you awake for it. They give you something to fuzz the edges, but you're still in there—watching, hearing, feeling. Kind of.

I walked into a freezing steel operating room lit up like a stadium, surrounded by masked strangers. A nurse handed me a gown and said to change behind the curtain. No underwear. No back. Just good luck. I sat on the metal table—bare and freezing—when a male nurse walked over with a razor. Not some sleek surgical trimmer. No, this was a single-blade, ten-cent gas station razor. The kind that causes chafing just by existing. He didn't say a word—just got to work shaving everything. And I mean everything. I sat there trying to play it cool while he silently prepped me like a Thanksgiving turkey.

Then they strapped me down like a psych patient and started threading wires into my veins. I drifted in and out of sleep for hours, waking up mid-procedure more than once—especially when they actually *burned part of my heart*. I remember screaming, "I need more meds!" but I couldn't move an inch. At one point I begged them to remove the oxygen tube from my nose because it was driving me insane. They finally did—mostly because I was snoring so loudly they figured I was fine.

The surgery itself went perfectly. They got it all. But the real fun came after.

Post-op, I had to stay completely flat for eight more hours to prevent clotting. And every single hour, Thelma and Louise—or whichever nurse duo was on shift—would stroll in, flip the blanket, flash me to the room, and check the incisions on both sides of my groin. They said it was medical. I'm still not sure. Because by the time all the shift changes were said and done, I'm pretty sure half the staff had seen the goods. I just lay there, trapped under fluorescent lights, wondering if this counted as trauma or comedy.

But the worst part wasn't the pain. It was the stillness.

Lying there, strapped in, bare, exhausted, I knew.

No fighter pilot gets cleared with a heart condition. No *Top Gun*. No dogfights. No Plan A. **Dream over.**

And honestly? That's probably when I officially decided school wasn't going to save me either.

Without that dream driving me, sitting in class felt pointless. Like I was wasting time playing by rules that didn't even apply anymore.

So I found the loophole.

Eighty percent of the grade came from tests, so why bother showing up all week?

Fridays were test days.

So I coasted Monday through Thursday, showed up on Friday, passed the test, and called it good.

And after heart surgery, it was *easy* to convince people I wasn't feeling well. The school didn't push back much—I had just been under the knife. And my mom? She wasn't trying to start a war. My older brother had already dropped out of high school, and she was desperate for me to at least make it to a diploma.

Eventually, she caught on to my routine. But instead of shutting it down, she cut me a deal:

"Keep a B average, and I'll write the doctor notes."

And just like that, I had a permission slip to skip the nonsense.

The system clearly wasn't designed for someone like me, so I stopped trying to fit the mold—and started figuring out what else I could build.

No more Plan A.

No clear future.

Just raw determination . . . and a growing list of side hustles that were about to change everything.

Plan B: The Marine Corps

Okay—so maybe I couldn't be Maverick.

But maybe . . . I could be General Clayton Abernathy.

Yeah, I know—technically, that's the name of a G.I. Joe character.

But I was born first, so . . . do the math.

Also, he was in the Army.

I had my sights set higher.

So I signed up. Got sworn in. Had my boot camp date locked. I even walked like a duck in nothing but my boxers to prove I was Marine material. You haven't lived until you've done squats in front of a government official while trying to keep your balance and your dignity at the same time.

It was happening. I was finally doing what grown-ups could point at and say, "Now that's a respectable young man."

I was *one month* away from reporting to boot camp.

And then . . . came the senior trip. Brighton, Utah. Snowboards. Five of my buddies. End-of-high-school celebration.

Three days on the slopes, and we were *this close* to wrapping it up.

But no one ever ends a trip without those famous last words:

"One more run."

And here's the kicker—*for some reason, I was by myself on that last trip down the mountain.*

No clue why. Everyone else was hanging back, maybe grabbing snacks or messing with their gear.

But me? I wanted one more ride.

It was quiet. Peaceful, even.

Just me, my board, the mountain, and the illusion that nothing could possibly go wrong.

And then—BAM.

Some guy launched off a jump like he was chasing a medal . . . and *landed directly on top of me.*

I didn't even have time to react.

One second I was cruising.

The next—I was on the ground, everything hurt, and I couldn't move.

That guy skidded to a stop and rushed over.

I remember him leaning over me, eyes wide. "Dude . . . Are you okay?"

I shook my head. "No. I'm not. I'm having trouble moving."

His face went pale. "Man, I can't be seen here. I work here. If they find out I hit someone—I'm fired."

And right there, flat on my back in the snow, I made a deal.

"Just stay with me long enough to get help," I said. "You don't have to stick around after that."

Because I knew—I wasn't walking off that mountain. Not fast, and definitely not far.

Snap—my neck was broken.

Crack—ribs shattered.

Crunch—shoulder destroyed.

And just like that, a surgeon was drilling a steel plate into my shoulder.

Thirty days from boot camp.

Somehow—*miraculously*—I wasn't paralyzed. But I wasn't going to be a Marine, either.

The Marines saw the medical report and said, "Thanks for your enthusiasm, but . . . no."

Someone told me, "Try the Army. They'll take anyone."

Even the Army said no. They took one look at my medical history—heart surgery, shoulder screws, a neck held together by duct tape and determination—and politely suggested I sit this century out. I told them I had grit, discipline, and a real desire to serve. They said I looked like a balloon animal that had been inflated, deflated, patched, and reinflated by an unsupervised child on a sugar high. At best, I was a backup party trick. At worst, a walking VA claim waiting to happen. So there I was.

Heart problem? Check. Steel shoulder? Check. Crushed dreams? Double check. Plans A and B? Vaporized.

At that point, I didn't have a direction. Just disappointment and a body full of metal. But here's the thing about losing everything you thought you wanted—you start looking at what you've actually got.

And somehow, all those odd jobs, side hustles, and weird little skills I'd picked up along the way . . . They started to matter.

They were seeds. Planted years earlier. The kind that don't bloom until you're standing on a job site, calling the shots, and realizing—you've already lived the training.

The truth is, gaining *skills* is the single most important thing you can do in life. It doesn't matter how old you are or what the skill is. Every skill you build becomes part of your tool kit—whether you're seven or seventy. You never know when you're going to need it. And you don't always see the value right away. But trust me: Nothing's wasted.

Because here's what nobody tells you when you're a kid: Every single skill counts. Even the weird ones. *Especially* the weird ones.

The ones that don't come with a certificate. The ones people roll their eyes at. The ones that feel silly in the moment—until one day, they don't.

Twisting balloon animals in a purple wig? Turns out, it taught me how to hold a crowd. How to grab attention. How to sell something people didn't even know they wanted.

Getting mistaken for a girl while clowning at birthday parties? That taught me how to take a hit, laugh it off, and keep performing. Thick skin. Quick wit. No ego.

Umpiring little league games as a kid with a high voice and oversized chest protector? That taught me how to lead with confidence, even when nobody takes you seriously at first. How to speak with conviction. How to make the call—right or wrong—and own it.

Working construction in the Tucson heat at sixteen? That taught me grit. That sometimes showing up and sweating is the most important skill you've got.

None of it looked impressive back then. None of it came with applause or LinkedIn endorsements. But those were the skills that built the foundation.

The weird ones. The quiet ones. The ones that didn't fit on a college application but ended up shaping everything I became.

So yeah. Especially the weird ones. Don't sleep on those. They're the secret weapons.

Chapter 5

Knives, Balloons, and the Fine Art of Faking It

By the time high school was wrapping up, I had a solid clown business going. I was making sixty-five dollars an hour and working around ten hours a week—not bad money for a teenager in face paint. But as much as I loved entertaining, I kept thinking . . . Do I really want my kids introducing me as "Snappy the Clown" one day? Was this really my long-term move? The answer, pretty quickly, was no.

I wasn't done performing—I just wanted a different stage. And dance had always been there in the background of my life, quietly waiting its turn. Before I was born, my parents ran an Arthur Murray studio—but it shut down long before I came along. Still, they never stopped teaching. They even tore out the shag carpet in our living room so my mom could keep teaching tap and ballet to neighborhood kids. I grew up watching rows of little feet shuffling across our floor while she clapped counts and corrected posture like a boss.

Naturally, I joined in. I took ballet and tap from my mom until I was about ten—right up until one of the kids at school saw me in tights. That was it. Done. Career over. I didn't want that kind of publicity. I wanted to dance, not get roasted on the playground.

Around the time I was five, my parents had enclosed the carport and turned it into a full-on dance studio. Mirrors, a barre, and black-and-white vinyl tile floors that clicked like Fred Astaire in a rainstorm. It wasn't fancy, but it worked—and for a while, it helped keep us afloat. By high school, the studio had become my bedroom. Same mirrors, same checkered floor. And that's when I really started dancing—ironically, when no one was watching. I'd spend hours in front of those mirrors teaching myself how to pop and lock with nothing but raw stubbornness and a stack of worn-out VHS tapes. My first instructors? *Breakin'*, and that scene in *Major Payne* where he busts out dance moves to impress the girl—because of course that's what love looked like in a nineties movie.

And let me tell you—there's nothing quite like trying to fall asleep in a room where your own reflection is just standing there . . . judging you. Shirtless. Confused. Lit by a single dusty lamp like it's about to file a report.

Eventually, I decided to take it seriously. My dad connected me with one of his old instructors—a guy who used to teach for my parents back when they ran their studio. When my parents stepped away from that world, he kept going. By the time I met him, he had his own successful studio in Tucson. And man, what a guy. He took me under his wing and taught me ballroom, Latin, even a little Western. He trained me for free—which was a huge blessing, because beginner dance teachers don't make much. You can only teach beginners, and beginners don't stick around long.

But the more I danced, the more I realized something: Yeah, I loved dancing. But I *really* loved teaching.

And that realization stuck with me. Over the next thirteen years, no matter where life took me, dance followed. Sometimes it was teaching, sometimes it was performing, and sometimes it was just cutting loose in the middle of a packed club. But it was always there.

At the same time I was getting into dance, I got a letter in the mail. It was from a place called Vector Marketing, and it was written like I was some elite recruit.

Now, I don't know who at Cutco wrote that letter, but they deserved a raise—and maybe a Pulitzer.

It showed up just a few weeks after I graduated high school. I was seventeen, sitting in the wreckage of every plan I'd made—no Marine Corps, no college scholarship, no clear future. My friends were planning dorm rooms and campus visits. I was trying to figure out how to rebuild from scratch.

Then this letter lands in my mailbox like a golden ticket.

We've heard about you, it said.

We think you're exactly what we need.

Come join our elite team.

It didn't just invite me to a job—it spoke to something deeper. Like maybe I wasn't just drifting. Maybe I still had potential.

They never said what the job was. But right there, in bold letters, was the magic phrase:

$15 an appointment.

At that point, they could've been selling ferrets in trench coats. I didn't care. I was in. "Yes. Absolutely. Whatever it is. Where do I show up?"

That's how I became a knife salesman.

The job was selling Cutco kitchen knives through in-home presentations—basically, I'd bring a briefcase full of blades into someone's living room, smile like I was on a game show, and try to convince them they couldn't live another day without the "Super Shears."

Now here's the kicker: The letter made it sound like I'd been handpicked. Like they'd scoured high schools across the nation, run a background check, interviewed my teachers, and landed on me. I felt chosen. Special.

Turns out? They send that letter to everyone.

If you had a pulse and could pronounce *cutlery,* you were halfway hired.

But I didn't know that. Not yet.

All I knew was that someone saw something in me. Even if it was a marketing ploy, it worked. Because at a time when every door had slammed shut, this one had flung open like it was meant for me.

And I walked through it—headfirst, heart full, knives in hand.

Now, here's the thing they don't tell you when you start with Cutco: It's really hard.

I thought I was going to be amazing at it. I mean, come on—I'd been clowning professionally since I was twelve. I knew how to juggle. I could make balloon animals on command. I wasn't shy. I wasn't afraid to perform.

How hard could knives be?

Well . . . Apparently, very hard.

I tanked my first few weeks. I did appointment after appointment, and the only thing getting cut was my pride. I wasn't selling much of anything, and I couldn't figure out why. I was charming. I was nice. I followed the script, mostly.

Nothing.

It wasn't until I got paired with Monique, the top seller in our office, that I realized I wasn't failing because I wasn't good enough—I was failing because I was overcomplicating it.

I tagged along to one of her appointments, and I watched this tiny, quiet girl absolutely dominate a homemaker set sale like it was nothing. She didn't do anything flashy. She didn't pull out dance moves or balloon swords. She just followed the script, asked for the sale, and smiled.

And they bought.

That's when it clicked for me: Oh. This isn't about tricks. This is about doing the work and asking the right questions.

So I did exactly that . . . with just a little of my own flair sprinkled in, obviously.

Now here's the thing—I was busy. I wasn't just selling knives. I was still clowning. I was still dancing.

Some days I'd go from making balloon animals at a kid's party straight to selling a thousand-dollar knife set to Mrs. Jones in her living room.

And if Mrs. Jones had kids? You better believe I brought balloons to that appointment. If Mr. and Mrs. Jones seemed a little stiff? I'd bust out a dance move I'd just learned. Was it part of the official Cutco script? Not exactly.

Did it work? Absolutely.

I wasn't the top salesperson, but I earned something just as good: respect.

People saw how much I was doing. They saw how hard I was working. And slowly, I started getting good. Three months in, just as I was finally finding my stride, Cutco came to me and said, "Hey, you're doing great. How would you like to run an entire office?" I said yes, obviously. I always said yes. So in 2001, at just eighteen years old— barely a year out of high school—I packed up and opened my first office in Santa Fe, New Mexico. I had no idea what I was doing. None. Find an office space? Sure. Hire people? I brought on two hundred in four months. Train a team? Why not.

We sold nearly two hundred thousand dollar's worth of knives in that tiny little town. At the time, I thought I was unstoppable . . .

And was also mildly disappointed. Because while I was grinding away in Santa Fe, I kept seeing these other offices pulling huge numbers, and I couldn't help but compare.

"Man, they're selling circles around me."

Turns out, I held the Santa Fe knife sales record until 2019—and if you adjust for the nearly fifty percent price jump by then, I'd still be holding that title today.

So, when they asked if I wanted to take over an office in Colorado Springs, I said yes.

And when they asked if I could cover Pueblo, CO, too? Sure. Why not.

Next thing I knew, I was running three towns, working sixteen-hour days, six and a half days a week, barely coming up for air.

And that's when I hit something I'd never felt before: burnout.

And not just the "man, I could use a day off" kind of burnout.

I'm talking the soul-sucking, brain-fried, body-aching, what-am-I-even-doing-anymore kind of burnout.

The kind where your whole system just . . . starts to shut down. But the pressure doesn't. The expectations don't. The work definitely doesn't.

So what do you do?

Well, I tried to outrun it.

Tried to grind harder, sleep less, care less—whatever it took. And when that didn't work, I started reaching for anything that would make the burnout feel less real.

I had never really touched drugs or alcohol growing up.

It's not that I was some perfect kid—I wasn't. But I stayed out of a lot of messes for one simple reason: My parents made a decision before I even existed. They both came from homes where addiction ruled everything. The kind of hurt that lingers for generations—unless you stop it.

And they did stop it.

Before any of us kids were born, they made a promise: *Our children won't grow up like that.*

And they kept it.

I never saw a beer in the fridge. Never saw a cigarette in the house. Never saw my parents drunk or high or out of control.

They didn't just break the cycle—they crushed it.

So when they warned me about addiction, when they told me their stories . . . I believed them. But I didn't *feel* them.

For a long time, those addiction stories felt like background noise—part of my family's past, but not part of *me.* I had goals. I had grit. I was working hard, chasing challenges, building something I was proud of.

But here's what I didn't understand back then: I'm wired for struggle. I *need* something to fight for. And when life got too easy—or when I couldn't see a path forward—I didn't feel relief. I felt restless. Frustrated. Like I was wasting my time if I wasn't pushing against something hard.

That's what made drugs so dangerous for me. They didn't feel like an escape at first. They felt like a way to *raise the stakes.* To make things exciting again. Sometimes it was boredom, sometimes it was burnout, and sometimes it was just that stuck feeling—like I didn't know where to go next. I didn't even realize I was setting fire to my own progress—I just wanted to feel that edge, that pressure, that fight.

At first, it was small—just enough to shake things up. Then a little more. Then more than that.

What I wish I knew back then is that you can learn to create challenge and excitement without leaning on addiction. But doing that? That's harder than anything else you'll ever do in life—especially if you've already tasted addiction.

The problem was, by the time I realized that, I was already in deep. The rush, the shortcuts, the constant need to feel like I was pushing against something—it had all worked . . . until it didn't. The very thing that kept me fired up had also hollowed me out. I wasn't chasing goals anymore. I was just chasing the feeling of being *in the fight,* even if the fight was with myself.

And that's the catch: When you build your identity around pushing through and out-hustling everyone, you don't really know what to do when the tank runs dry. I had pushed and pushed until there was nothing left to give. No fuel. No purpose. No direction.

And that's when it all caught up with me.

So when the moment finally came—when I woke up and knew deep down that I was **completely spent,** with nothing left in the tank—I picked up the phone, called my manager, and said, "I'm done. I can't do it anymore."

And I meant it. Every word.

This wasn't frustration talking. It wasn't a bad day or a rough week. This was the full weight of burnout, addiction, exhaustion, and emptiness crashing down all at once. I'd hit my wall. There was no pushing through this one.

No mission.

No momentum.

Just the sinking thought that maybe I'd already peaked.

Maybe that was as good as it was ever going to get for me.

But here's what I see now that I couldn't see back then:

I did an *incredible* thing.

I achieved the highest personal level in Cutco sales. I opened a successful branch and district office. I was part of the number one division in the world for knife sales—in the largest knife company on the planet. That's not small. That's not a failure.

Did it go how I thought it would? Not even close.

I shot for the stars . . . and didn't quite make it.

But I landed on the moon—and gained experience I couldn't have gotten any other way.

And that matters.

Because no matter how messy or imperfect it looked from the inside, those years built a foundation I didn't even realize I was standing on.

So before we move on, I want to do something I haven't really done yet in this book. I want to zoom in—not just on the story, but on the *lessons* inside it.

Because this next chapter? It's not just about selling knives.

It's about what selling knives taught me—about people, about pressure, about performance, and about what it really takes to close the gap between effort and success.

So let's break it down.

Chapter 6

Cutco Sales 101: Lessons from the Knife Game

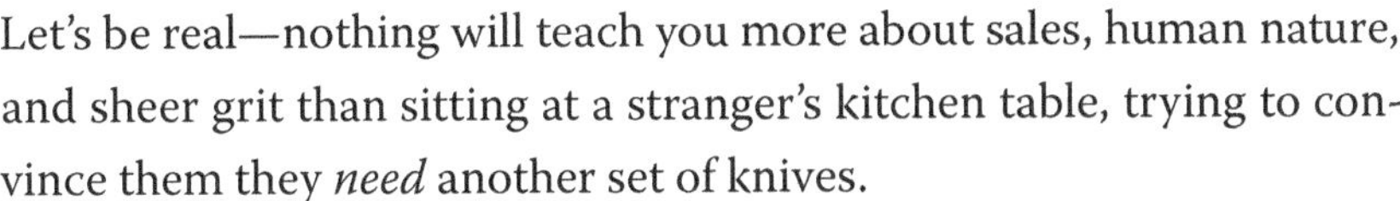

Let's be real—nothing will teach you more about sales, human nature, and sheer grit than sitting at a stranger's kitchen table, trying to convince them they *need* another set of knives.

Those two years with Cutco? Easily one of the best business educations I've ever had. Sure, they gave me a script—but real life doesn't follow a script. You learn fast that people are weird. Some are suspicious. Some are too polite to kick you out. Some just want to see you chop a penny in half and then send you on your way.

I learned what makes people buy, what makes them hesitate, and what makes them say yes even when they swore they wouldn't.

And honestly? I learned how to eat rejection for breakfast, lunch, and dinner—and still show up smiling the next day.

And before you skip ahead, thinking, *Well, I'm not in sales*—let me tell you something straight:

Yes. You. Are.

You're always selling something.

Your idea. Your value. Your vision.

Your solution. Your experience. Your story.

You sell when you walk into an interview, when you pitch a client, when you lead a team.

But it goes even deeper than that.

You're selling when you're raising your kids—teaching them right from wrong, showing them how to believe in themselves, convincing them vegetables won't kill them.

You're selling in your marriage—building trust, staying connected, reminding your spouse you're still choosing them.

You're selling to your friends—when they're on the edge and need your belief to stand a little taller.

You're even selling to yourself—every time you get out of bed and decide to keep pushing forward.

So no—you don't get to sit this one out.

The people who know how to sell—how to lead, how to connect, how to build trust and move people—those are the ones who build lives that matter.

They raise strong families.

They lead powerful teams.

They start world-changing companies.

So this chapter?

It's not about knives. It's not even really about Cutco.

It's about learning how to communicate. How to influence. How to lead.

It's about the five lessons that shaped the way I do business, raise my family, and show up in every room I walk into.

These lessons gave me leverage in every industry I've ever touched.

And if you let them—they'll do the same for you.

Lesson I: Believe in Yourself and What You're Selling

Before anyone buys your product, your idea, or even your advice . . .

They buy **you.**

That's the first sale.

It's not about what you're selling—it's about **who's selling it.**

Because people don't buy from people they don't trust.

And trust doesn't come from a script. It comes from how you carry yourself. From who you are.

You can have the best product in the world. You can rehearse the pitch, memorize the stats, and even show up in a suit with shiny shoes and perfect hair.

But if people don't believe in you, they're not buying.

That's why belief matters so much.

You have to believe in what you're offering.

Because **belief is contagious.** When people see that you mean it—that it's real for you—they start to lean in.

I'll never forget one of my early Cutco appointments.

This sweet older couple invited me into their home like I was their grandson. They offered me lemonade, let me sit at the kitchen table, and listened to my whole pitch—start to finish. I gave it everything I had. The jokes. The charm. Even a balloon animal for their grandkid. I was nervous, but I believed in what I was doing.

And when I finished? They smiled and said,

"That was very nice, but I think we're okay. We don't need any knives right now."

I nodded and started packing up—trying not to let the disappointment show on my face. But before I could close my sample case, the wife leaned in with this little grin and said,

"You're not going to leave here without a sale, are you?"

I blinked. "I guess not?"

She turned to her husband. "We don't need knives," she said, "but we like *him.* Let's buy something."

They didn't buy the big set. They bought a little paring knife and a trimmer. But to me? That was everything.

It wasn't about the knives.

It was about the connection. The trust. The belief.

They believed in **me**—and that mattered more than the pitch, the product, or the price.

That sale taught me something I've never forgotten:

When people believe in you, they'll give you a shot.

Even if they don't need what you're selling, they'll find a way to support you—because **trust creates movement.** And movement leads to results.

And this goes way beyond sales.

You've got to believe in your parenting.

You've got to believe in your marriage.

You've got to believe in your mission.

You've got to believe in yourself.

That means doing the work.

Wrestling with your values. Learning what actually matters to you. Testing your convictions.

Because if you don't fully believe in something, don't try to sell it—

Not to customers.

Not to your team.

Not to your spouse.

Not to your kids.

Not to yourself.

Do the work until it's **real.**

When your words and your life line up—people feel it.

That's when the trust shows up.

That's when the sale happens.

So yes—belief in the product matters.

But belief in **you** comes first.

Lesson 2: Ask for the Sale, Then Shut Up

Here's a hard truth most people in business (and life) never learn:

If you don't ask, you don't get.

And I don't mean *hint* at it.

I don't mean *circle around it.*

I mean **ask for the dang sale.**

When I first started, I was terrible at this. I'd give the full presentation—crack jokes, juggle knives (kidding . . . kind of), make balloon animals for the kids—then completely freeze at the finish line.

Instead of asking clearly, I'd say stuff like:

- "So . . . What do you think?"

- "Want to sleep on it?"

- *"Let me know if you're interested . . ."*

Translation? *Please reject me gently; I'm fragile.*

That's not how you close.

The Golden Rule: Ask for the sale—then shut up.

That's it. That's the move.

- "I think this set is perfect for your kitchen. Should we go ahead and write it up for you?"

Then I zip it. No rambling. No backpedaling. No awkward explanations.

Just let it sit in the air.

And here's the magic:

Whoever talks first . . . loses.

It's not about pressure—it's about confidence.

You've shown the value. You've done the work.

Now respect them enough to make a decision without begging or hovering.

Silence is where the "yes" happens.

This isn't just about sales.

This rule applies to everything:

- **Want a raise? Ask.**

- **Want to delegate something? Ask.**

- **Want your kid to own a decision? Ask—then pause.**

If you keep talking, you're not helping—you're sabotaging.

And if you're afraid they'll say no? That's okay.

Ask anyway.

Because confidence doesn't mean you're not nervous.

It means you believe in what you're offering.

So yes—**ask for the sale.**

Then shut up.

And let the silence do its job.

Lesson 3: Rejection Is Your Best Friend (And People Actually Want to Say Yes)

When I first started selling Cutco, I took every no personally.

Like I'd failed.

Like they were saying no to me—not the product.

But then I learned one of the most important (and freeing) truths in business and in life:

People love to buy. They just hate being sold to.

Nobody wants to feel pressured. Nobody wants to feel manipulated.

But **everyone** loves walking away with something they feel good about—something that solves a problem or makes their life better.

That's why I never wanted to be "the sales guy."

I wanted to be the trusted guide. The one they celebrated with when they found something they genuinely wanted.

So I did something simple—but powerful:

I made it okay to say no.

No pressure. No awkward silence. No guilt-trip.

And guess what?

When people feel safe to say no, they're a whole lot more likely to say yes.

Because the truth is . . .

People suck at saying no—so they make up lame excuses.

Some of my all-time favorites:

- "I need to check with my spouse."

(Even though their spouse hasn't cared about kitchen knives in twelve years.)

- "I never make big decisions on the spot."

(Says the person who bought an eight-hundred-dollar elliptical they now use to hang laundry.)

- "I'll think about it and call you later."

(Translation: "This conversation is over.")

At first, I took these at face value.

Then I realized: most nos aren't really no.

They're just fear. Or hesitation. Or a need for more clarity.

A no is really just a request for more information.

Every rejection is just someone asking for a little more confidence before they say yes.

So I started answering the unspoken questions before they ever had to ask.

I gave them all the reassurance they needed. And surprise—sales started rolling in.

Rejection isn't the enemy. It's the blueprint.

And here's the thing—this isn't just true in sales.

It's true when you're raising kids.

It's true in marriage.

It's true every time you put yourself out there with an idea, a dream, or a request.

Rejection isn't a wall. It's a mirror.

It shows you what isn't working, what needs work, and what could be done better.

At home, I've learned the same principle works with my wife and kids.

Sometimes when they push back, they're not saying no.

They're saying, "Help me understand," or "I'm not sure I trust this yet."

And if I slow down, listen, and lead with clarity instead of control—things go a whole lot smoother.

So whether you're selling knives, pitching a deal, leading your family, or trying to convince your kid to eat broccoli—rejection is your friend.

Because every no is just one step closer to the right kind of yes.

And if you're willing to listen, learn, and adjust—you'll get there.

Lesson 4: Referrals Are the Real Goldmine

Your best customers aren't the people you know.

They're the people your people know.

Once I understood that, my entire sales strategy changed. I stopped stressing about finding new leads and focused on the ones sitting right in front of me—**happy customers with friends who trust them.**

I made it my personal rule:

Never leave an appointment without at least ten referrals.

And no, I didn't beg or awkwardly fumble through it.

I made it easy—almost fun—for people to refer me.

How I made referrals easy for people:

- **Instead of asking,** "Who do you know?" I asked, "Who loves to cook?"

It got their brain going in the right direction. Specificity matters.

- **I gave them a number to hit.**

"Most people give me at least ten names. Let's see who comes to mind."

Now it's a challenge, not a chore.

- **I didn't stop at names**—I asked for filters.

"Who on this list is most likely to buy?"

Qualified referrals saved me hours of wasted time.

And once I got good at this?

I never cold-called again.

No more awkward intros. No more dialing strangers who didn't want to hear from me.

Every appointment came with built-in trust—**because someone they knew had already vouched for me.**

This Isn't Just Sales, It's Life

Think about it.

Your best opportunities?

They've almost always come from someone who believed in you.

A job lead from a friend.

A business deal from someone who heard you were the real deal.

Even relationships—How many of us met our spouses, our best friends, our key employees, **because someone made an introduction?**

People trust people who are trusted.

So whether you're growing your business, building your family, or trying to raise your kids with the right influences—**referrals still matter.**

- Surround your kids with good mentors? That's a referral.

- Meet someone great because your friend vouched for them? That's a referral.

- Land a dream client because someone said your name in the right room? Referral.

Your network is your shortcut.

Your reputation is your resume.

And the people who believe in you are your sales team—whether you asked them or not.

So stop chasing strangers.

Start multiplying trust.

Lesson 5: The Sale Happens in the Room (So Does the Trust, the Breakthrough, and the Win)

If they don't buy when you're there, they probably never will.

That's not pessimism—it's real.

Because once the moment passes, so does the momentum.

They forget how they felt.

They second-guess what they saw.

They get busy, distracted, pulled into life—and the clarity disappears.

That's why I stopped walking out of appointments without getting real.

If someone gave me a soft maybe, I'd lean in and say,

"Hey—this isn't just a nice way of not having to say no now and making it easier to do it over the phone later, right? It's totally okay to say no now if you want."

Then I'd smile and add,

"Or, let's just fill out the order you **do** want, and I'll have it ready for you."

What surprised me was how often people appreciated the honesty. It lowered the pressure, broke the tension, and gave them space to make a real decision.

And more often than not? That little nudge turned a maybe into a yes.

It felt bold at first. But people respected it.

Because deep down, people don't want to waffle.

They want someone to lead them with confidence.

Not pressure. Not manipulation.

Leadership. Clarity. Truth.

Because here's what most people don't realize:

When you close in the room, they don't just buy—

They remember *why* they bought.

The emotion is fresh. The decision is clear.

They're anchored in the "why."

And that means it *sticks*.

Same thing happens in life.

Because this isn't just about selling knives.

This is about marriage. Family. Leadership.

That hard conversation with your spouse?

That moment with your kid when they're actually listening?

That breakthrough idea you finally have the courage to pitch?

Don't put it on a calendar. Close it in the room.

Because when you do—it lasts.

They remember the tone. The trust. The feeling of being seen and understood.

They remember *why* they changed their mind.

Why they softened their heart.

Why they decided to believe again.

But if you wait?

If you walk away and hope they "circle back"?

That moment you were praying for?

It's gone.

So yes—**ask for the sale.**

But also ask for the moment.

Ask for the connection.

Ask for the decision that could change everything.

And when the time comes?

Don't stall. Don't overthink. Don't talk yourself out of it.

Close. In. The. Room.

Final Thought:
Master These 5 and You'll Never Starve

If you can learn how to:

- Build trust

- Handle rejection

- Ask for the sale

- Leverage referrals

- Close in the room

you'll never go hungry. In business, in relationships, in life—you'll always find a way forward.

For two years, Cutco was my training ground. It gave me real-world tools I still use to this day. It taught me how to connect with people, how to handle pressure, how to move through fear and take action anyway.

But there was a flip side, too.

Because I didn't leave those two years untouched.

I came out stronger, yes.

Smarter, sharper, more confident—yes.

But I also came out tired. Burned out. Running on fumes.

And somewhere along the way, I'd picked up a few habits I couldn't shake.

A little partying to take the edge off.

A few drinks to unwind.

Some stuff I said I'd never touch—until I did.

I never planned on becoming someone who needed something to cope.

But slowly, I started leaning on things I didn't fully understand.

And when the pressure finally cracked me, I didn't have the tools to fix it.

Chapter 7

Mexico: Because Why Not Just Move to the Party?

Burned out? Check.

Fresh off running three Cutco offices? Check.

No clue what I was doing with my life? Big check.

So naturally, when my friends invited me to Mexico for a twenty-first birthday bash, the only reasonable answer was "Absolutely, let's go."

And this wasn't just a "Hey, come for the weekend" kind of invite.

No, this was "Dude, you're coming. No excuses. You're one of us."

And when it's **Deva's** birthday? You show up. Yes, that's her real name.

She was one month older than me, and the best way to explain Deva is this: She just loves people. She's the sister you choose. The kind of person who finds the good in you and brings it out like it was never lost. Being around her made you feel seen. Known. Better.

And then there was **Kenny.** Kenny was like Deva in some ways—warm, magnetic, quick to laugh—but man, this guy knew how to party. He was tall, bold, fearless, and always on the lookout for the next big deal. I met Kenny through Cutco. He was already a manager while I was still in the Tucson office, and he'd picked up a lot of the same skills during his run there. Kenny didn't just think outside the box—he sold the box to someone else and partied with the profits.

I met Deva through Kenny, and it was through the two of them that I met **John.**

John just fit. A little more reserved than Kenny or me, but he didn't need to be loud—he had the looks, the calm confidence, and the kind of energy that made people lean in when he talked. He was smart, kind, and always down for an adventure.

The trip had more people, sure—maybe nine or ten in total—but the core crew was the four of us. And let me say this: the others were amazing too. Every single person brought something special to the trip—humor, energy, heart. But for time's sake, we'll stick with the main crew.

We all piled into one big, white van. Not just any van—this thing had history. It used to belong to an old high school, and you could still see the faded outline where they'd peeled the school logo off the side. It hadn't been refurbished or cleaned up. It was exactly like it had been back when kids were getting dropped off for football practice. Deva's dad—who had a reputation around Sierra Vista for buying all the forgotten junk in town—had picked it up for cheap, and somehow it still ran. It wasn't the kind of van that screamed *bright future*, but it had windows, a blue racing stripe, and a whole lot of character. Crammed in shoulder to shoulder, bags on our laps, music blasting from someone's half-broken speaker—we were headed straight into what felt like the best decision of our lives. And here's what made this crew so special:

We were all alphas. All leaders. All driven. The kind of people used to calling the shots and having the last word. And you'd think that would've been a recipe for chaos—but it wasn't.

Because underneath all that ambition, we shared something more important: we wanted to get better. We weren't competing *against* each other—we were competing *with* each other, pushing each other to rise higher.

We listened to each other. We never tried to outshine or over-power one another. We definitely talked each other into some ridiculous things—but it was never out of ego. We were building momentum together.

A whole study could be done on how we got along. And honestly? That study would baffle people.

Deva was a vegetarian Democrat.

Kenny and John leaned more Republican.

And I was a straight-up Libertarian.

We talked about everything—religion, politics, all the stuff you're not supposed to bring up at dinner. But instead of getting defensive or angry, we'd just go, "Huh. Okay." And that was it. No lectures, no debates. It was like we mentally bookmarked it: *Good to know. That's part of who they are.* No judgment—just curiosity.

And honestly, none of it ever really mattered. We *loved* those parts of each other. We celebrated the differences. We could go deep on faith, values, or who we were voting for, and it never got ugly. We respected each other because we knew—deep down—that if you took away any one of those parts, the person wouldn't be the same. And none of us wanted that. Not for ourselves, and definitely not for each other.

Because the real win wasn't agreeing.

It was belonging.

And for the first time in my life—I truly felt like I belonged.

We rolled into Rocky Point like we owned the place.

Kenny and I basically threw some shorts in a bag and called it good. We didn't wear shirts back then. And if, by some chance, a shirt *did* make an appearance? Oh, you better believe it was unbuttoned. Fully open, chest out, wind blowing through what little hair I had—like we were starring in some low-budget beach movie no one asked for.

That was the look.

That was the vibe.

That's what the girls liked.

And if we were going down, we were going down in style.

Sunburnt? Didn't matter.

Hair a salty mess? Only added to the effect.

Tanned, reckless, and running on zero plans, we strutted through Rocky Point like we had cracked the code. And for a little while, it felt like we had.

We partied.

We laughed.

We caused a ruckus that would've made our high school teachers weep.

And somewhere between the beach bonfires and the late-night street tacos, Kenny—turned and said,

"Dude . . . We should stay."

And somehow, that was all it took.

I had some money saved up from my Cutco run.

Kenny did most of the legwork.

And before we knew it . . .

We weren't just **visiting** Mexico anymore.

We lived there.

We went back to the US for a few days to grab more clothes, and by the time we came back down, Kenny had already found us a place to stay and hustled up a way to work real estate deals. We weren't just stretching a vacation. We were starting a whole new chapter.

Before the money ran out, though, there was one story that still makes me laugh, even now.

When we were trying to hustle real estate, we needed signs. You can't sell beachfront property without signs. So Kenny and I tracked down a local metalworker who supposedly made custom ones. We showed up every few days to check in, and every time it was the same answer:

"Mañana."

Tomorrow.

Always tomorrow.

Weeks went by. Still no signs. Still *mañana*.

At first, we laughed. Then we got annoyed.

But we kept showing up—too many times, apparently.

Because one day, instead of handing us our signs . . .

He called immigration on us.

We were back at the real estate office—probably planning our next pitch—when two very serious men in uniform walked in.

Mexican immigration.

They weren't there to talk.

They were there to investigate.

They started asking questions fast.

And I mean **fast.**

Kenny and I looked at each other like, *Uh oh . . . This might be it.*

And then, like a gift from above, it turned out a powerful Mexican attorney just happened to be in the office that day. He stood up and calmly told them we weren't employees—we were just hanging around, learning the business.

Whether they bought it or not, they let us go.

But they made one thing crystal clear:

"If we catch you working here without the right paperwork, we'll throw you in jail long enough to teach you a lesson . . . and then drop you off at the border."

Message received. Loud and clear.

Next day?

Passports and visas. Immediately.

Lesson learned: Never underestimate the word *mañana*.

And always know who's watching when you're hustling property abroad.

But the real problem wasn't immigration.

It was money.

And that lifestyle we were living?

It burns through savings faster than sunscreen on a spring-breaker.

Soon, the party started to fizzle, and reality set in.

We were broke.

That's when **survival mode** kicked in.

And for me, survival looked like . . . balloon animals.

Yeah.

While other people were hustling timeshares or bartending for tips, I reached back into my clown bag—literally—and brought out my old party trick.

Kenny? He was my hype man.

He'd warm up tables at restaurants, get people laughing, and the next thing you know, I'm standing there in a half-buttoned shirt, twisting up a balloon giraffe like our lives depended on it.

(Because they kind of did.)

We worked restaurants.

We charmed the tourists.

We smiled like we weren't one bad night away from splitting a single plate of nachos and calling it dinner.

And somehow, we made it work, for a little while.

Because really, we weren't chasing money.

We were chasing a **feeling.**

That feeling of freedom.

That feeling of belonging.

That "no one's telling us what to do" magic that made it seem like we'd hacked the system.

But here's the thing about that kind of freedom: If you're not careful, it turns on you.

The late nights stopped being fun.

The drinks stopped hitting the same.

And the people we thought were just like us?

They started to look . . . tired.

A lot of them weren't down there for freedom.

They were down there because they had nowhere else to go.

Some were running from something.

Some were just running.

And that's when it hit me.

I wasn't living the dream. I was getting my first real glimpse at the nightmare my parents had warned me about. For the first time, I understood why my mom prayed so hard. Why my dad never drank. Why they looked so concerned when I brushed off their advice.

Because under all the sun, sand, and party lights . . . there was a darkness. And I was standing way too close to the edge, looking down and thinking, What if I just leaned a little further?

And then I started to notice something else.

I wasn't doing things for joy anymore. I wasn't chasing adventure.

I was chasing numb.

I drank to feel looser. Smoked to slow the thoughts down. Hooked up to feel wanted. Partied to forget why I was so tired all the time.

What started as freedom turned into a new kind of prison. Because I was no longer bound by rules, expectations, or responsibilities . . .

I was bound by addiction.

Addiction to escape.

Addiction to the next hit of excitement.

Addiction to feeling *something*—anything—that wasn't the weight of aimlessness.

And I told myself I was free.

But I was anything but.

I was finally untethered from the world that burned me out . . .

But now I was tethered to the very things that were burning me from the inside.

That's what scared me the most.

I wasn't living the dream.

I was just keeping the darkness quiet.

And just when I was thinking I might tip all the way over . . .

I met her. Sarah.

And suddenly, I had a way out. A new plan. A new city. A new life. And I took it.

Chapter 8

From Beaches to Britney Spears

Leaving Mexico wasn't easy, but it wasn't dramatic or loud. There was no teary goodbye, no blazing argument—just a slow realization that if I stayed, I'd lose myself.

And then, like a door opening at the exact moment I needed it, there was Sarah.

Young. Gorgeous. The kind of gorgeous that turned heads in every room—sometimes too many. Guys would walk up mid-conversation and try to shoot their shot, like I was her little brother tagging along instead of the guy she came with. She didn't just look like Britney Spears—she looked like the version of Britney that made you pause mid-scroll on MTV and forget what you were doing. Early 2000s Britney. Before things got messy.

And me? I was still messy. Still carrying sand in my shoes, balloon animals in my past, and addiction in my bones. But Sarah didn't see that. Or maybe I didn't let her. Either way, she looked at me like I could be someone. Like I already was.

So when the chance came to leave Rocky Point behind and start over in Phoenix? I took it.

Sarah wasn't just a girl—she was my escape hatch. My validation. My new plan. And if it meant chasing her to a new city, reworking my entire life, and rebuilding from scratch? So be it.

Phoenix: The High Life

Phoenix felt like redemption. Clean streets. Real jobs. No fear of immigration or running out of balloon giraffes.

I got my real estate license fast. Signed on with New Home Information Center. During the day, I showed houses. In the afternoon and evenings, I was teaching ballroom dance full-time at Fred Astaire. At night, we hit the clubs with the other instructors, dancing until the floorboards groaned.

And for once, I wasn't burning out.

I was flying.

There was rhythm to my days. Money in my pocket. A girl on my arm. I'd wake up thinking, *This is what life's supposed to feel like.* I was on my way to the life the world promised would make me happy—a beautiful girl, money, and being seen.

I had arrived.

Looking back now, I can see that I'd already done some pretty incredible things by that point in my life. I wish I'd been able to acknowledge that then—to actually feel proud of what I'd built. But for some reason, I couldn't. It's like I still had something to prove. I don't know if it was because I grew up so poor, always feeling like the kid who didn't belong. Maybe that's why I was chasing the life the world said would make me happy—the beautiful girl, the money, the attention. As if proving I'd made it would finally quiet the old voices in my head.

Sometimes I wonder if I was trying to prove them wrong—or prove the world wrong. I'm still not sure. All I know is, even in my best moments, I felt like I was racing some invisible clock. Trying to outrun the doubt. Trying to become someone I could finally be proud of.

But if you'd asked me then? I'd have said everything was perfect.

I could see my future—and I believed I was going to have it all. The girl. The money. The success. The fame.

The Wedding That Wasn't

Sarah was fun. Spontaneous. Up for anything.

I mean, you'd have to be. She met me in Mexico, and the next thing you know, we're planning a wedding. Most people date for a few years. We dated for a few months and dove in headfirst. No hesitation.

That's the kind of relationship it was—fast, intense, built on chemistry, adventure, and that intoxicating feeling that maybe—just maybe—we were rescuing each other.

She was wild, beautiful, and ready to build a life.

I was broken, addicted, ambitious, and still dragging the dust of Mexico behind me.

But I think she saw something in me. Something buried beneath the chaos. She looked at me like I was the man I could be, not just the mess I was carrying. And part of me believed she might be right.

We were opposites in a lot of ways. But we made it work. At least, for a while. She tried to do both—bring out the better version of me and keep up the crazy pace we were running at. But you can't live two lives forever. Sooner or later, one catches up with the other.

And just when it felt like we were about to make the leap into something permanent . . .

Three days.

That's how close we were to getting married.

The venue was booked. The rings were bought. We had a plan for everything—except the part where her mom would step in and blow it all up.

Apparently, after some last-minute research, Sarah's mom discovered I'd been raised Mormon.

Not that I was going to church. Not that I was preaching. Just that I had grown up that way.

And that was all she needed.

She convinced Sarah to back out—and instead of calling me, Sarah's mom called my mom.

Let that sink in.

Three days from "I do," and I didn't even get the breakup call. My mom did.

One minute, I was rehearsing our first dance. The next, I was standing in my kitchen wondering if the last year had even happened.

And yeah, it wrecked me.

Not just because I lost the wedding. But because I had bet everything on that life. On her. On us. On the idea that maybe this was my clean break from the past. My second chance.

And in one phone call—it was gone.

What hurt the most wasn't even that I'd been judged for something I wasn't doing—it was that I'd been disqualified for something I was born into. A label I never claimed. A faith I never pretended to practice.

The truth is, I hated being called a Mormon—not because of the people or the doctrine, but because I didn't want to give anyone the wrong idea. I didn't want to represent something I wasn't living. I didn't want to give it a bad name. And I didn't want people thinking I was something I never really understood.

Sarah's world saw my upbringing as disqualifying. But to me, it was just part of the story. A piece of my past that I wasn't even trying to defend—just live beyond.

But here's the thing: Sarah was right about me. As much as I hated being called a Mormon, as much as I wanted to outrun the label, the truth is, it was in me. The way I'd been raised, the idea of God, of church on Sundays, of right and wrong—it was woven into who I was, whether I acknowledged it or not. I hadn't yet learned how to carry that part of me without dropping everything else I was trying to hold.

The world we were building together crumbled in an instant—which, in hindsight, saved us both a ton on catering.

What do you do after that?

You move forward. What else is there?

The wedding was off. The girl was gone. The plan was shattered.

And I was left standing in the rubble, trying to figure out what to do with myself.

I could've unraveled. Slid back into old habits. Found the nearest bar and made some new mistakes.

But I didn't.

Because even though I'd lost the plan, I hadn't lost the lesson.

When life pulls the rug out from under you, you land however you can. And I was done with the free fall. I'd seen where that leads. I'd lived it.

So I leaned into the one thing that had always been there when everything else fell apart: the grind.

No more distractions. No more shortcuts. No more pretending.

It was time to figure out real estate for real.

And that's exactly what I did.

Chapter 9

The First Big Flip: The Deal That Changed Everything

By the time I was twenty-one, I'd already thrown myself into a handful of big ideas. Some worked, some didn't. But real estate? That one had its hooks in me early.

I wasn't new to the game at this point—I'd been showing homes, learning contracts, talking to builders, and asking way too many questions at every sales meeting. I knew the language. I knew the hustle. I was gaining confidence, getting sharper, and beginning to see the business not just as a job—but as a vehicle.

But up to that point, I'd still been playing it pretty safe. Working for others. Making commissions. Getting the reps in. What I hadn't done yet? Taken a swing of my own.

That changed in Chandler, Arizona.

At the time, I was living and working in the East Valley Phoenix area. Chandler, a small outskirt town of Phoenix Metro, was booming. The 202 freeway was nearly done, major companies were flooding in, and Chandler Fashion Mall had turned into the crown jewel of the region. Everything about it screamed growth. If you were paying attention, you could feel it. It was the kind of place you wanted to buy in before everyone else figured it out.

So that's what I decided to do.

There was just one tiny problem: I had no money. Like, none.

But here's the thing about me—I've never let something as small as being broke stop me from making a big decision. I believed in the opportunity. I believed in my ability to hustle. And deep down, I believed I could figure it out.

So I started driving neighborhoods near the mall, looking for anything with potential. Fixers. For-sale-by-owners. Burnouts. You name it. I was hunting.

That's when I found it.

A 3,200-square-foot home that smelled like it had been marinated in soy sauce and regret. The previous owners had run a Japanese restaurant, and let's just say . . . the fish had followed them home. On top of that? Bright-green carpet. Like, cartoon-lawn green. You couldn't miss it.

But I didn't care. Because the smell? Replace the carpet, scrub the surfaces, open the windows—gone. The location, though? Couldn't be improved. It was exactly where I wanted to be.

So I locked it up.

I got the house under contract for three hundred and fifty-five thousand dollars.

There was just one hitch—probably the biggest red flag I've ever ignored in my entire life: the contract required **proof of funds within twenty-four hours.**

And I had absolutely no funds to prove.

I stared at that clause like it might change if I blinked fast enough. I couldn't show a bank statement. I couldn't fake a line of credit. All I had was belief and a very real ticking clock.

So I went into overdrive.

I started calling everyone I knew—friends, old coworkers, my barber's cousin's neighbor—anyone with a pulse and a checkbook.

Everyone said no. And I mean **fast.**

I had put earnest money down, and it was about to vanish. I was one "sorry, man" away from learning an expensive lesson.

Then the phone rang.

It was **Brian Davidson.**

Now, I didn't know Brian well at the time. But I knew his name. And more importantly, **he had money.**

Turns out, my mom had been bragging about my real estate hustle to someone in the grocery store (as moms do), and word made its way to Brian. He called me up out of the blue and said,

"Tell me about this deal."

So I pitched it. I laid out the comps. Talked about the freeway expansion. The mall. The upside. I even told him about the fish smell and the carpet—I wanted to be real with him.

He listened. Paused. Then said,

"I'm in."

Just like that.

We secured **one hundred percent financing** and closed the deal.

A year later, that house appraised for **six hundred and twenty thousand dollars.** We didn't just walk away—we turned that profit into a whole lot more.

Let me tell you something: when you're twenty-one, and you just made more money on one deal than most people make in five years?

That **changes you.**

That deal didn't just inflate my bank account—it rewired my brain.

Suddenly, the idea of making thirty thousand dollars a year in some salaried job felt laughable. I saw what was possible. I tasted it. And I wanted more.

The Flip That Flipped Everything

That deal wasn't just a win—it was the win that proved I wasn't crazy for believing in myself. It taught me something I hadn't felt in a long time: I was capable. Not just of working hard or following a script—but of creating something. Building something. Trusting my gut and being right.

It's hard to explain what that feels like when you've been running for years—chasing validation, craving a moment that tells you,

"Yes. You've got what it takes." Because up to that point, I'd always been *almost.*

Almost successful.

Almost secure.

Almost enough.

When the numbers cleared and I saw the profit sitting there—it hit deeper than just dollars in the bank.

It felt like *proof.*

Proof that I wasn't just some washed-up kid from Tucson with a wild past and a few decent stories. Proof that I could see something before it was obvious. That I could step into the unknown and actually win. And it wasn't just for me, either.

It felt like I was finally becoming the man I'd always told people I was working toward. The man I hoped my parents could be proud of. The man I'd promised Sarah (although she was gone) I was becoming. The man my younger self would look at and say, "See? We made it."

It was more than a flip.

It was a turning point.

Showing the Win

And after that deal hit, I couldn't wait to show my family—not the check, but the life.

It wasn't about flexing money or tossing keys like a movie scene.

It was about the house. The neighborhood. The fact that for the first time, I had something real to show for all the chaos I'd pushed through.

I remember when my parents came to see the house. Big corner lot. Fresh stucco. New windows. It wasn't extravagant, but it was solid. Clean. Beautiful in the way that says, *We're not just getting by anymore.*

And my siblings came too—Jesse, Mya, Scott, Tania.

We all walked through that house together.

I watched them step onto the tile, look around the kitchen, run their hands across the granite. I watched my dad nod slowly, quietly. My mom smiled, but not the kind of smile you throw on for pictures—this one was deeper. Like something heavy had finally loosened in her chest.

They were proud. I could feel it.

But I could also feel the quiet prayers behind their eyes.

Because as proud as they were of how far I'd come, they were still praying I'd let go of some of the things I'd picked up along the way. The habits. The crowd. The inner chaos.

They never said it. Never shamed me. Never tried to steal the moment.

They did what great parents do.

They celebrated the win—loud and sincere—and prayed in their closets for everything else.

And honestly, that made me love them even more.

Because they never stopped believing I could turn the corner.

And they never stopped showing up for me, even when I was still figuring out how to show up for myself.

It wasn't just a house.

It was *proof.*

That the sacrifices they made weren't wasted.

That all those prayers my mom whispered when I was off the rails didn't disappear into the ceiling.

That even the kid who once gave out pay phone numbers as his "home number" could build a place worth coming home to.

And as we stood there—my whole family under that one roof—it felt like a line had been drawn in the sand.

This side?

This was new.

This was the start of something better.

The Momentum

After that, the deals didn't get easier—but I got **stronger.**

I started to move differently. I walked into rooms with a new kind of confidence—not cocky, but grounded. I knew what I was capable of, because I'd done it.

I'd made something real happen.

And that momentum became my oxygen.

One flip turned into two. Then five. Then ten. Each one stretched me. Taught me something new. Pushed my limits in a way no boss or job ever could.

But more than that?

They healed me.

Every successful deal patched something I hadn't even realized was broken. Every dollar earned from something I built with my own hands and vision started to silence that voice in the back of my head that said, *You're just pretending.*

This wasn't just about real estate.

This was me reclaiming ownership over my life.

I could choose the projects. Choose the risks. Choose who I partnered with, how I ran things, what I stood for.

It was the first time I felt like my life belonged to **me.**

So yeah, this deal changed everything.

Not just because of the money.

Not just because it made me a player.

But because it was the moment I stopped surviving—and started building.

And looking back, I'm glad my parents got to see it.

Not just the house.

Not just the numbers.

But the shift.

The weight that came off my shoulders.

The proof that all their sacrifices—the late nights, the grocery store coupons, the whispered prayers behind closed doors—had built something real.

I wasn't showing off.

I just wanted them to feel what I felt:

That it worked.

That we'd made it.

That even though I didn't follow the map they might have imagined, I was still getting us there.

They never reached the kind of financial freedom I was stepping into.

But because of them, I could.

And I would carry that torch further—because of everything they gave up to keep the fire going.

Not just for me.

But for them.

And the best part?

I was just getting started.

Chapter 10

Greed Is Good . . . Until It Isn't

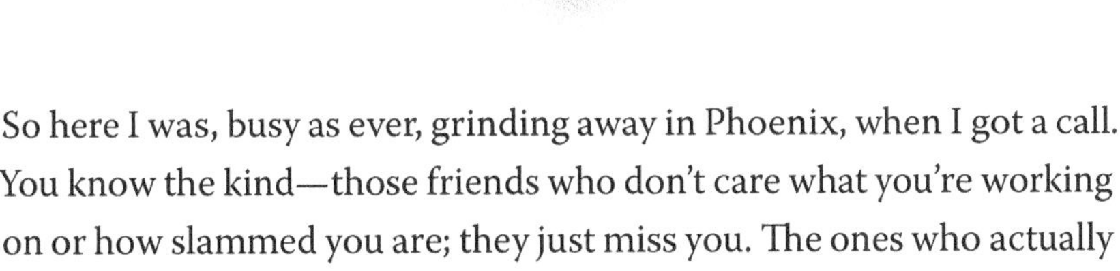

So here I was, busy as ever, grinding away in Phoenix, when I got a call. You know the kind—those friends who don't care what you're working on or how slammed you are; they just miss you. The ones who actually love you, not for what you're doing, but just for who you are.

And yeah, sure, we'd definitely done some sketchy stuff together over the years, but honestly? They taught me more about real friendship than just about anyone else. So when they said, "We're heading back to Mexico," there wasn't a question in my mind.

The rest of the crew was making a trip down to see Kenny—and I needed to be there. Not just because it sounded fun (which, of course, it did), but because those were my people. My chosen family. When they called, I showed up. That's just how it worked.

And man, Mexico never disappointed. Back then, it wasn't just a getaway—it felt like stepping into this wild, lawless playground where nothing mattered except having a good time. And my friends? They knew exactly how to make that happen.

Almost every night, we'd end up in some packed dance club, and like clockwork, they'd shove me right into the middle of the floor.

Empty dance floor? No problem. They knew I'd get it moving. It was like my unofficial job—kickstart the party, get the energy up, and before long the whole place would be jumping

Dancing was like my secret weapon back then. Total cheat code. The music would hit, and I'd turn into a human firework—arms flying, feet sliding, the whole floor waking up like someone just yelled, "Free tacos!" No warm-up. No hesitation. Just instant ignition. And yeah, it definitely helped that girls noticed. I mean, what's not to like about a guy who could moonwalk in jeans like a discount Michael Jackson?

But the real fun wasn't about flirting—it was about flipping the whole vibe. I'd start the party, my crew would jump in like backup dancers who never rehearsed, and suddenly we were running the room. The DJ would crank the volume, the lights would hit just right, and boom—we owned it. And when we left? We weren't just leaving— we were leading a full-blown parade of bad dancing and even worse choices through the streets of Mexico, like Mardi Gras met spring break and forgot to pack a plan.

I didn't even notice her at first.

I'd already done my thing—hit the floor, got the room moving, pulled off a few spins that probably would've impressed Michael Jackson's cousin. The crowd was hyped, the DJ was finally playing something worth dancing to, and that's when I spotted her.

And right in the middle of one of those nights—lights flashing, music thumping, sweat flying off someone's forehead—I was mid-spin, probably halfway through a Michael Jackson lean that only works if no one looks too closely, when I noticed her.

She was dancing with Kenny.

At first, I figured she was just some random tourist who got swept up in our chaos. Happens all the time. But then I saw the way she moved—not just with the beat, but with confidence. Like she wasn't trying to catch attention . . . She just *had* it.

Then it clicked—this wasn't some random girl. She was with the crew. She'd come down with Tara, Deva's little sister. And by the way Kenny was grinning and goofing off with her, it looked like she was already part of the family.

Kenny and I pulled a full-blown *Night at the Roxbury* on her—both dancing on either side like the awkward, overconfident idiots we were. She laughed, shoved us off, rolled her eyes, and kept dancing anyway.

Eventually, she drifted my direction. I cracked a joke. She threw one right back. I tossed a sarcastic line. She volleyed it without missing a beat.

We danced for a while—not that slow, awkward kind of dancing where you're pretending not to care. This was the kind of dancing where you're both trying to outwit each other with footwork and sarcasm. It was playful. Easy. No pressure. No agenda.

Eventually, we peeled off from the crowd and found a quieter corner of the club, still loud enough to shout over the music but tucked far enough back to pretend we were having a real conversation.

She asked where I was from. I told her Phoenix, but that I'd just come off a stint living in Mexico. She raised an eyebrow.

"Wait—you *left* Mexico, and now you're *back* in Mexico? You realize that's not how vacation works, right?"

I laughed. "I'm not on vacation. This is a reunion tour."

That made her laugh, which made me want to keep the conversation going. I asked about her story—she was from Sierra Vista, had grown up around strong women, was sarcastic enough to hold her own in any crew, and had a way of saying things that made you feel like you'd known her longer than you had.

There wasn't some dramatic moment. No epic, sparks-flying, slow-motion realization. Just . . . comfort. Like we spoke the same language. And by the time the night ended, we'd both kind of agreed—without really saying it—that we were going to see each other again.

We didn't do the "I'll call you" game. We just said, "This was fun. Let's do it again." And a few days later, we did.

The next time we hung out, it wasn't in Mexico. No neon lights, no clubs, no parade of half-dressed spring breakers following us through the streets. Just two people trying to figure out if there was anything real underneath all that energy.

She came up to Phoenix.

We swam at my house, stayed up too late playing double solitaire, and laughed at how competitive we both got over a card game that no one else on the planet even played. It wasn't fireworks—it was something better. Familiar. Comfortable. Like slipping into your favorite hoodie after a long day.

And just like that, it became a thing.

We'd trade weekends—her in Phoenix, me in Sierra Vista. It started casual, but slowly, almost without meaning to, it got serious. We were texting every day. Talking late into the night. Laughing at inside jokes that no one else understood. You know the kind.

The kind that makes you think, *Huh . . . Maybe this is something.*

I didn't mean for it to get that way. I had told her up front—I wasn't looking for a relationship. I'd just been through one that tore me up, and I wasn't exactly eager to step into round two. But love has a funny way of ignoring your plans. And before I knew it, I was doing all the things a guy *not looking for a relationship* does—buying her little gifts, introducing her to my friends, even thinking about what a life with her could look like.

And if I'm being honest, I didn't give Lia my all right away. I kept it light on purpose. After everything with Sarah, I wasn't exactly sprinting toward another crash-and-burn.

But when Lia said, "I love you," everything shifted.

That moment flipped a switch in me. I thought, *Okay . . . If she's going all in, I should at least try to meet her there.* If I could give my heart to Sarah—if I could plan a wedding, dream up a future, and take that kind of risk—then I owed it to Lia to show up with the same energy.

So I did.

I leaned in. I gave her more of me. My time. My focus. I let her into the world I was building—deal by deal, day by day. I made space for her in my life and started thinking about what "us" could look like long-term.

And once that thought settled in . . . I couldn't shake it.

And my brain? Full shutdown.

Because I liked Lia. A lot. But I'd been in love before. I'd been wrecked before. So hearing those words again? It hit like a car crash and a warm hug all at once. Confusing. Terrifying. Kind of beautiful.

And the wild part?

I said it back.

Not because I was ready. Not because I had it all figured out. But because I meant it. As complicated and tangled and guarded as I still was, there was a part of me that believed her. That wanted it to be real. That hoped maybe, just maybe, this was the beginning of something that wouldn't fall apart.

And in that moment, I was all in.

I wanted it to work. I *wanted* to believe this one was different. That this could be the thing I built instead of another thing I had to survive.

But slowly, quietly, I started noticing the cracks.

Little things she'd say.

Moments when the sparkle in her eyes didn't feel like it was about *me*—but more about the image. The lifestyle. The idea of being with someone who was young, ambitious, and already "making it."

And the more I paid attention, the more I couldn't shake the feeling: *She doesn't love me. She loves the idea of me.*

She could've plugged in any guy who was doing what I was doing and told the same story. That kind of love—the "plug-and-play" version—terrified me.

Because I've never been good at pretending. And I definitely wasn't going to build a future on a fantasy.

We were having one of those deeper conversations—one of those "what really matters to you" kinds of talks—and I asked her how she felt about her dad.

Not casually. Not as a test. Just . . . curious.

And her answer?

"I respect him."

That was it. Not "I love him." Not "He's my hero." Not even a soft memory or a story. Just respect.

And for some reason, that hit me hard.

Because love, to me, had always been bigger than respect. Messier. Warmer. More forgiving. Love wasn't just earned through deeds—it was lived in the details. In showing up. In grace. In trying, even when it's ugly.

And I remember thinking, *If that's how she sees the man who raised her . . . what does that mean for the man she chooses?*

It made me feel sad, honestly. Sorry—for her, for that kind of love. A love that was measured in discipline and duty, not in warmth and connection. And deep down, I was scared that same version of love would eventually leak into what we had.

That maybe one day, she'd look at me and say the same thing.

Not "I love him."

Just "I respect him."

And I knew—I couldn't live with that kind of love.

I grew up watching people fall in love . . . and then fall out just as fast. I didn't trust it. So I started testing her. Subtle stuff. Just to see if she loved me or if she loved the version of me with a house and a checkbook.

She passed a few of my quiet tests. Enough for me to keep going. But deep down, I still wasn't sure. I couldn't shake that voice whispering, *Is this real . . . or just convenient?*

And here's the thing—by this point, I'd already run a few businesses. I'd felt the highs, the wins, the rush of everything working. But I'd also lived through the lows. The silent phones. The deals that fell through. The moments when momentum vanished and confidence got real quiet. And one thing I knew for sure: No matter how good you are, you don't stay on top forever.

So if I was going to commit to someone, I needed to know they could ride those waves. That when the applause stopped and the grind got messy, they'd still be there. I didn't need a cheerleader when things were easy—I needed a partner when things got hard.

So I decided to strip everything back.

I moved back to Tucson. No fancy house. No money show. Just me, living at my parents' place, trying to figure out what was real.

Lia still lived in Sierra Vista, and I'd go up there to see her. We kept things going for a bit. But I was watching closely now. Trying to see what she really saw when she looked at me.

Meanwhile, I needed to keep working. I wasn't about to sit around waiting for clarity—I needed a new play. And that's when I looked up John Flemming.

We'd met back in Mexico—John had been selling real estate out there, and we'd crossed paths enough times for me to remember he had a license and a little newspaper business in Tucson. He wasn't flashy. Definitely not high energy. But he had tools I could use, and I knew how to build with whatever was in my hands.

So we grabbed lunch. Then another. Next thing you know, we're sketching out a plan in his run-down kitchen, surrounded by cracked tile and potential.

And I told him straight-up, "I think we can do something big here."

Now, I don't really know how to do things small. Never have. So after a few sketchy lunches and a couple whiteboard sessions that were really just napkins and Sharpies, I pitched him on the bigger picture.

He had a broker's license and a tiny newspaper. I had the energy, the experience, and a playbook full of ways to turn scraps into systems. So I said, "Let's build a real estate school."

It wasn't just an idea. It was a strategy.

Most brokers wait around for licensed agents to come knocking— people who already have habits, baggage, and their own way of doing things. But I had a different thought: What if we trained them from the very beginning? What if we built the habits, the mindset, the work ethic—before the bad ones had a chance to settle in? I hadn't seen it done, but I could see what it might become.

What if we trained people from scratch?

What if we created our own agents, taught them the right way from day one, and built a team that understood our system?

We'd use the newspaper to generate leads. Sell ads. Push listings. Then, we'd funnel all that momentum straight into the school. People would come in for the paper and leave with a career path.

John was into it. At least, enough to say yes.

So we made a deal: I'd run the recruiting, the ad sales, the growth. He'd provide the infrastructure. Fifty-fifty split.

Simple.

And as usual, people doubted me.

But within a few months, that tiny newspaper? Went from a thousand copies to nearly fifty thousand. Agents were signing up. Ads were flying. And right when that school license finally cleared, I filled the seats.

Just like I said I would. It worked.

The newspaper was humming. The school was buzzing. I was in full builder mode—doing what I do best. Momentum. Vision. Growth.

John seemed happy. Agents were excited. Students were showing up, learning, getting licensed. I was back in my element, waking up every morning with purpose and a packed calendar.

And sure, it was stressful—there were still all-nighters, hiccups, and things breaking behind the scenes. But I'd built enough systems by then to know how to stay ahead of the curve.

It felt like we were building something real. Something that could scale.

But little by little, I started noticing a pattern.

Every time we had a win—every time a big commission landed, or a record number of students enrolled—John and his wife would hit me with this weird little phrase like it was an inside joke:

"Greed is good. Greed is great. Greed will help you motivate."

First time? I chuckled. Thought maybe it was just their version of a pump-up line.

Second time? I raised an eyebrow.

By the tenth time? I started thinking maybe I should check my pockets before leaving their house.

And deep down, I knew. That little voice in my head—call it instinct, intuition, or just the ghost of deals past—started yelling, *This is going to blow up. Handle it. Now.*

But I didn't. Because I was young, and they were older and "wiser" and had a printer in their living room, which apparently made them professionals.

So I ignored it. I told myself I was being paranoid. That maybe I was the problem. That if I just worked harder, they'd come around.

Spoiler alert: They didn't.

And if there's one lesson I've learned the hard way, it's this:

That voice in your gut? That's your board of directors. And when it calls an emergency meeting, you better show up.

Nowadays, when I feel that inner nudge that something's off, I don't wait. I hit that problem like it owes me money. I go full ninja-accountant-meets-Rambo. I solve it before it becomes a PowerPoint slide in a lawsuit.

But back then? I let it ride.

And the universe? Oh, it cashed in that bet real quick.

So yeah, I ignored the red flags. I let it ride. Kept telling myself, *Clay, just keep working. People see the results. They'll do the right thing.*

One day, John calls me in. I'm thinking maybe we're reviewing numbers, maybe finally talking about growth, maybe—I don't know— getting lunch that doesn't come from a gas station.

Instead, he hits me with this:

"Clay . . . I don't think you're worth fifty percent anymore."

Now, I don't know what face I made in that moment, but inside? My soul hit the brakes so hard it left tire marks.

I built this thing. I was the recruiter, the salesman, the marketer, the janitor, the motivational speaker. I was literally doing everything but physically printing the paper myself with a Sharpie.

And this man—this *floating-on-a-paper-license, hasn't-hustled-since-Nixon* man—wanted to renegotiate?

Nah.

At first, I tried to process it. I was like, *Okay, maybe this is a joke. Maybe Ashton Kutcher's about to jump out and tell me I've been Punk'd. Maybe we've slipped into a sitcom where betrayal happens before the first commercial break.*

But no.

This dude really looked me in the face, after watching me turn a half-baked newspaper into a full-fledged business, and said, "You're not worth it."

So I did the most logical thing I could think of.

I walked.

Didn't yell. Didn't throw a chair. Didn't even take the leftover donuts I'd brought for the team.

I just nodded, stood up, and left.

And then?

Every single agent I'd brought in left too.

Like a dramatic scene in a Netflix series—me walking out the front door, and behind me? A whole parade of agents, files, and middle fingers.

Because John thought I was just the spark.

He didn't realize I was the whole engine.

And once I unplugged?

That thing choked, sputtered, and face-planted harder than your uncle doing karaoke on roller skates.

Part of me wanted to say, *I told you so.*

But honestly?

I didn't have time.

Because while John's ship was sinking, *my* personal *Titanic* was getting ready to crack in half too.

Because here's what that whole mess taught me: When someone shows you who they are, believe them. And when they show you twice? Run. Or better yet—moonwalk out while making eye contact, just so they know you're not coming back.

I'd done my part. I built something real. And I left with my peace.

But life has a funny way of handing you back-to-back tests—like it wants to see if you really learned the lesson the first time.

And just as I was walking away from one kind of betrayal . . .

I was walking straight into another.

Enter: Lia.

Here's the part I haven't mentioned: I'd gotten engaged. Bought a ring. Tried to get sober. Not because she asked—but because when I pictured a future, I saw kids. And when I saw kids, I thought about my dad.

My dad came from hell. But somehow, he didn't drink. Didn't do drugs. He told me once, "I did the best I could. Your job is to better it." That line stuck.

So I tried.

But here's the thing—I didn't really quit. I tried to quit. Which basically meant I quit for a few days . . . until Lia asked me to drink. Or there was a party. Or someone handed me a joint with that "don't be lame" look. And boom—I was right back in it.

Trying to change while staying in the same environment? That's like trying to dry off in the middle of a rainstorm. Not just any rainstorm—like sideways rain, shirt-sticking-to-your-skin, thunder-shaking-your-guts kind of storm. No umbrella. No coat. Just you, standing there with a paper towel, hoping for a miracle.

That's what quitting felt like.

I was trying to get clean while still showing up to the same places. Same friends. Same rhythms. Still walking into rooms where weed was normal and beer was just part of the conversation.

And nobody was shoving anything down my throat. That's what made it harder. It was all "Come on, just one," or "You've been doing great," or my personal favorite: "You're more fun when you're high."

And the worst part? They weren't wrong.

Weed slowed me down. I'm high-strung—big shocker, I know. When I was high, I was slower, dumber, easier to deal with. I liked myself better that way. So did a lot of people. Including Lia.

But when I got clean—even halfway clean—I got intense. Focused. A little sharp around the edges. And maybe that wasn't what she signed up for.

One night, we had a date planned. Nothing fancy—just dinner and a chance to talk, to reconnect. And I remember actually being hopeful. Like maybe we'd turned a corner. Maybe we were building something again.

But she never showed.

No call. No text.

Just . . . gone.

I sat there for hours, telling myself she must've gotten stuck. Maybe her phone died. Maybe something came up. I refreshed my texts a dozen times like that was going to change anything. Eventually, I drove back home. Alone. Confused. A little embarrassed. A lot heartbroken.

I waited another day. Still nothing.

So I did what any semi-reasonable person would do—I called a mutual friend. Not to pry. Just to make sure she was alive.

"Oh yeah," they said. "She's fine."

That was it.

No explanation. No apology. Just the emotional equivalent of a door slammed in my face.

And man . . . That stung.

Not just because she bailed. But because I had let her in. Really in. Past the jokes. Past the hustle. Past the guy who could fill a dance floor or close a deal. She got the version of me that was trying to grow up. Trying to change. Trying to be a man worth staying for.

And she dipped.

No conversation. No "This isn't working." Just silence. Like I'd never been anything more than a weekend fling who'd overstayed his welcome.

I'd love to say I shrugged it off. But I didn't. It wrecked me more than I expected.

Because I thought I was getting better. I thought I was building something. I thought maybe, this time, it would stick.

Instead?

It vanished. And left me standing there with a ring that had been returned and a bunch of questions that never got answers.

And for a while, I just held on to it.

I didn't rush to the jewelry store. I didn't want to believe it was really over. Some part of me still held on to the hope that maybe this was a phase. Maybe she'd call. Maybe we'd talk it out. Maybe the ring would still mean something.

Because truth be told—it was perfect.

I picked it out with my whole heart. Simple. Elegant. Classic. It wasn't the most expensive ring in the store, but it was thoughtful. I chose it like I was choosing the future—carefully, hopefully, fully believing it would last.

But as the days passed, that quiet little box started to feel heavier than it should've.

It wasn't holding a ring anymore.

It was holding everything that didn't work.

So finally, I took it back.

I walked into the jeweler, placed it gently on the counter, and said, "I need something a little more reliable."

The guy gave me a look—half sympathy, half "yep, seen this before"—and offered me store credit.

So I picked out a watch.

Not too fancy, but solid. Dependable. Something that wouldn't fall apart under pressure.

And from that day on, I called it my **"Don't Be Stupid with Girls"** watch.

Because every time I looked at it, I wanted to remember: Don't lose yourself to win someone else. Don't confuse potential with partnership. Don't drop three months' rent on a promise that only one of you plans to keep.

That watch didn't just tell time.

It told the truth.

Spoiler alert: I eventually gave that watch to someone else.

Because one day—I didn't need it anymore.

Final Thought

Greed and love—two of the most powerful motivators in the world. Both can build empires. Both can burn them down. And in this chapter of my life, I watched both happen—back to back.

I don't regret any of it.

Because losing Lia and walking away from John taught me something I couldn't have learned any other way: You can't build a life that lasts with people who are only in it for themselves.

The good ones stay when the spotlight turns off.

The right ones double down when the deal gets hard.

And the real ones? They never ask you to shrink so they can shine.

And I wasn't going to shrink anymore.

So yeah—I left the girl. I left the partnership. I walked away from the whole house of cards.

Because somewhere deep down, I knew something better was coming.

Something I was meant to build. Something that wouldn't crumble under pressure or change its mind when things got hard.

And I wasn't going to waste another ounce of energy trying to prove my worth to people who couldn't see it.

This chapter didn't break me.

It refined me.

It taught me to trust that quiet voice in my gut. To move quicker when the warning signs flash. To notice who claps when you win—and who disappears when you don't.

And sometimes? It reminded me in small ways.

Like every time I glanced at my "Don't Be Stupid with Girls" watch and thought, *Right. Got it.*

Because the real deal was still ahead.

Chapter 11

Welcome to the Game

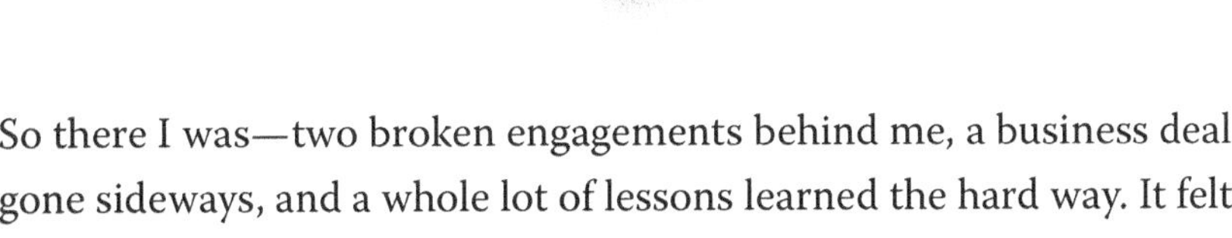

So there I was—two broken engagements behind me, a business deal gone sideways, and a whole lot of lessons learned the hard way. It felt like everything had fallen apart at once.

But the crazy part? Somewhere in the middle of all that chaos, I realized I'd picked up some pretty incredible tools. Through all the heartbreak and betrayal, I had actually figured out how to build something real.

I didn't just learn how to survive in real estate. I learned how to win.

And since you're here, reading this, I'm guessing you're looking to win too.

Before we move on, I want to pause and give you the playbook. This isn't theory. This isn't some recycled advice from a YouTube video. This is exactly what worked for me, boots on the ground, when I had to rebuild from scratch.

Now, just to be clear—this isn't where I *learned* how to sell.

That came earlier—from twisting balloon swords at birthday parties, teaching dance lessons into the late nights, and selling knives sharp enough to make Mrs. Jones smile.

This?

This is where it all came together.

Because even though this chapter is *technically* about selling real estate—it's really about something bigger.

It's about how to take everything you've learned from life—every hustle, every heartbreak, every weird job you thought would never matter—and use it to serve people well.

To show up with confidence.

To build trust fast.

To create momentum when everything feels stuck.

So no, this isn't *just* for realtors.

This is for anyone building something.

Anyone who needs to earn trust, grow their network, or turn their skill set into something that actually pays.

It's not about houses.

It's about people.

And if you care about people?

This chapter's for you.

The investing side—flipping, rentals, passive income—all that good stuff? We're getting to that later. But before you can play that game, you need cash flow. You need deals. You need momentum.

And that's what this is.

This is how I made real estate work for me when I needed it most. And if you're willing to show up and do the work? You can do it too.

I. Show Up Every Single Day

The best thing I did when I got into real estate was show up—every single day.

The service businesses aren't for the faint of heart or for anyone who expects things to just "happen" because they signed a piece of paper and got a business card. No, I showed up. And I didn't just show up like everyone else—I showed up early, stayed late, and hit the pavement hard when others were cooling off.

I wasn't the smartest. I wasn't the most experienced. But what I did have was a commitment to work my tail off, every single day.

Showing up isn't just about being physically present. It's about consistency. It's about setting expectations—and making sure you hit them.

It's about saying, *You can count on me. I'll be there. I'll deliver.*

But here's the part a lot of people miss: Showing up also means showing up *well*.

I couldn't afford a fancy car when I started. But the car I had? It was spotless. My clothes were sharp. My presentation was on point. Because a messy car, sloppy clothes, or a halfhearted pitch? That's a chink in your armor, and people notice.

When you show up, you're not just selling a product. You're selling confidence, professionalism, and readiness—whether you realize it or not.

I went from learning the ropes to pulling them with intention—showing up, doing the work, and figuring things out while others were still stuck at the starting line.

Because just standing around the ropes doesn't make you great. You have to climb them, pull them, and sometimes tie your own knots. That's what made the difference.

And that? That's what paid off.

2. Ask More Questions Than You Think You Should

Let me tell you, I didn't know what I was doing when I first got into real estate. Not a clue.

But here's the deal—asking questions was my superpower. I asked anyone and everyone. I didn't care how dumb the question sounded. I needed to know how to write a contract. How to talk to clients. What the market was doing.

And here's the kicker: Asking lots of questions helped me remember more. The more I asked, the clearer things became.

I also let my clients know right from the start that I wasn't afraid to ask questions. I told them straight-up, "If I don't know something, I'm going to ask. But I promise you, I will find the answer and make sure you're covered."

It wasn't just about asking questions to make sure I was doing things right—it was also about getting to know my clients. I would tell them, "I'm going to ask you a lot of questions, and I want you to feel comfortable answering them. I want to know what you like, how you feel, what's important to you. I'm here to find the house that fits you— not just the one that fits the budget."

I wanted to fall in love with the house at the same time they did. The only way to do that? Really understand what they were looking for. I wasn't just a salesperson trying to close a deal. I was there to connect, to find that special place that felt like home to them.

The more you ask, the faster you learn. And the more you learn, the better equipped you are to help your clients. So ask away. The people around you know things you don't, and when you ask, you're showing that you want to learn, not that you're lazy.

I remember getting into my first sale and realizing I didn't even know what some of the terminology meant. But instead of pretending I had it all figured out, I went straight to the people who did—the experienced agents and brokers around me. I asked questions constantly. I didn't care if I sounded green. I wanted to understand how they thought, how they solved problems, and why they made the decisions they did. I soaked up everything I could, like a sponge. That's how I learned—not just the technical stuff, but how the business *really* worked.

And because I wasn't afraid to ask, I didn't just pick up information—I learned how to listen. And that skill became my edge with clients. I knew how to ask the right questions, how to read between the lines, and how to respond in a way that actually moved the conversation forward. Asking taught me to listen, and listening taught me how to lead.

3. Outwork Everyone Around You

Here's the real secret—hard work beats talent. Every time.

When I first started, I wasn't the best agent. Heck, I was far from it. But I was the guy who kept showing up, kept learning, and most importantly, kept working harder than everyone else.

You can have all the training, the scripts, the perfect marketing plan—but if you don't put in the hours, you're just another face on a bench ad. The ones who break through? They *outwork* everyone around them.

If I didn't have a deal, I was out with flyers and posters. If I ran out of flyers and posters, I was researching free ways to advertise. If I didn't have anything else to research, I was asking other agents if I could tag along on their appointments—just like Monique taught me back in the Cutco days. And if no one would let me?

Then I'd light myself on fire and stand on a corner.

Not literally. But in Cutco, they used to say, "The best way to get people to notice you is to light yourself on fire—everyone wants to see what's going on."

And for me, that mentality never turned off.

I lived by a code: **ABS—Always Be Selling.**

It didn't matter where I was—open houses, gas stations, barbecues, weddings, even parties. If there were people, there was potential. I wasn't walking around with a clipboard and a pitch, but I was always tuned in. Listening. Smiling. Building relationships.

Everyone else might've been there for a good time—me? I was there for the deal hiding behind the good time.

Because I'd already learned: The couch won't close a sale.

Neither will silence.

You've got to get out in the world, let people feel your energy, and remind them that when they need someone they can trust—you're the one they remember.

I worked weekends. I stayed late. I followed up on every lead.

I worked when people were sleeping. I worked when people were relaxing.

And that's why it worked.

4. Build Your Network—And Keep Building It

Real estate is a people business.

The most valuable thing I did was build my network. I wasn't just focusing on selling houses; I was meeting people, forming relationships, and building a reputation. I networked with mortgage brokers, contractors, home inspectors, anyone who could refer clients my way.

But here's the biggest part of building your network, the one thing ninety-nine out of a hundred realtors won't do: Call and text every number in your phone. Yes, I said every number—not just the ones you know.

If you're on fire, you want everyone to know it. Those people you've met, no matter how distant, want to see you succeed, and they want to show you off. I'm talking about calling your old friends, acquaintances, that person you met once at a party—everyone.

This one thing is the most powerful form of advertising anyone can do, and yet, it's the one thing most agents steer clear of. Why? Because it's scary. It's easier to hide behind ads and social media posts, but it's the personal connection that really makes the difference.

The truth is, those who know you are more likely to refer you. When you call them, you're giving them a reason to be part of your success story. You're making them feel like they're in on the action. And when people feel like that, they want to be part of what you're doing.

And for the ones who don't want to see you succeed? You've got the perfect line to let them know you're going places: "I told you this was a good thing!" Let them see the grind, the hustle, and the success, and you'll leave them with no choice but to respect the journey.

Now, don't just call them—stay in touch with them. Ask about them; genuinely care about them. If you say you'll call someone tomorrow at eight p.m., make sure it's not 8:01. Honor your word. Show them that you value their time as much as your own. The follow-through is everything. People will remember you for being reliable, consistent, and someone they can count on.

The only time I would do any other marketing was when there was no one left to call. But trust me, if you're doing this right, that day will rarely come. You should never run out of people to reach out to.

5. Don't Be Afraid to Fail—And Fail Fast

Here's the cold truth: you're going to fail.

But the trick is to fail quickly, fail often, and learn from it.

I messed up plenty of times, and there were deals that fell through. But every time something went wrong, I learned. I made it a point to fail faster and learn from it so I didn't make the same mistake again.

If you're not failing, you're not learning. And learning is the only way to grow.

Now here's the kicker—your friends and family are going to tell you that you suck. Yep, they're going to tell you that you're stupid for even trying. You're going to hear it from the people closest to you. They'll try to pull you back into the comfortable, predictable life you've always known. But what they don't realize is that they're like crabs in a bucket.

You know the story, right? You throw a bunch of crabs into a bucket, and as one starts to climb out, the others will grab on to it and pull it back down. That's how most people operate. They see you trying to climb, to get out of that "bucket," and they don't want to be left behind. They want you to stay small, stay like them, because it's uncomfortable to see someone break out of the mold.

The crabs will always try to pull you back into the bucket—don't let them.

Instead, learn to recognize your failures. When you fail, take a second to learn from it and then move on. Even better? Learn to recognize the signs before they start coming up again. As you keep moving forward, you'll get better at seeing when things are about to go south—and you'll be ready to pivot.

Make more mistakes in a week than everyone else will in a lifetime. That's how you get better. That's how you learn. Don't be afraid to mess up—just do it faster and smarter next time. The more mistakes you make, the more you grow. And trust me, if you're not making mistakes, you're probably not trying hard enough.

6. Keep Your Ego in Check

Look, this is real talk—**Life should humble you.**

The more success you see, the more you think you've got it all figured out. But the moment you let your ego take over, you're one mistake away from losing everything.

I started closing deals and thought I was untouchable. Then came a client who proved me wrong. The second you think you know it all is the second you stop growing.

And please—don't be that agent.

If I had a rubber band for every agent who's started their spiel with "I've been in this business for ____ years, so I know blah, blah, blah"— I'd have a slingshot big enough to launch myself into orbit. Honestly, don't ever be that agent.

Ego kills deals. The more you think you know, the less you're willing to learn. People can smell arrogance a mile away, and clients don't want to hire someone who thinks they have it all figured out. Stay humble. Keep learning.

In real estate, humility goes a long way. Keep learning. Keep listening. If you're always trying to be the smartest person in the room, you're missing out on all the things that can take you to the next level.

7. Never Get Commission Breath

Never get commission breath.

What's commission breath, you ask? It's when you're so desperate for a deal, so hungry for that paycheck, that your clients only matter so you can get paid, and they can smell it a mile away. They'll feel it in your urgency, your pressure, and your need to close the deal. And guess what? They'll run.

Clients can always tell when you're too focused on the sale. It's like a sixth sense. And when you're desperate, they can sense it. No one wants to buy from someone who is more focused on getting paid than helping them. It's a huge turnoff.

Now, here's the hard truth—if you're broke, this is going to be tough. If you're living deal to deal, you're going to be tempted to push clients into decisions they're not ready to make, just so you can pay the bills. And that's where things go south.

The best way to avoid commission breath? Cut costs. Save money. Build up enough savings so you can go without a commission for at least six months. This gives you the breathing room to do your job without desperation clouding your judgment. If you're counting on a closing to pay your rent, guess what: That closing is probably not going to happen. Life has a funny way of making sure it doesn't work out when you need it to the most.

If you want to be successful, you have to remove the pressure from every deal. When you don't need the commission, you can relax, give your clients space, and serve them better. When you're not counting on every paycheck to make ends meet, you're free to do your job the right way.

That's how you build long-term success—don't chase the money; let the money chase you.

8. Keep Moving

Here's the thing—real estate never stops.

You can't afford to get comfortable or take breaks. There's always another deal to close, another client to meet, another opportunity around the corner.

I didn't stop after my first deal. I didn't stop after my first year. I kept pushing, grinding, and growing. Because in real estate, the moment you stop moving forward, someone else will.

Just keep moving. Keep learning, keep building, keep pushing, and you'll get to where you want to be.

9. Put Your Money Where Your Mouth Is

Here's a hard truth that a lot of people miss in this business: If you're trying to sell something, you better have skin in the game.

If you're out there selling real estate as an investment, you better be investing in it yourself. You can't just talk the talk and expect people to believe you. If you're trying to sell a fixer-upper, you better have rolled up your sleeves and fixed one up yourself. If you're pushing a multiplex to a client, you better have owned one—or at least have experience with it. People can tell when you're just reading from a script versus when you've lived it and believed it.

Clients aren't going to take you seriously if they feel like you're trying to sell them on something you've never done before. How are you going to advise them on investment properties if you've never made an investment yourself? How are you going to tell them about the joys and challenges of flipping a house if you've never touched a hammer or swung a paintbrush? You can't.

You must walk the walk.

If you're talking about flipping houses or buying rental properties, the only way you can really connect with your clients is by having experience doing those things. And not just the surface-level knowledge—really know the process. Know the headaches, the wins, the losses, and everything in between.

And here's why: credibility.

Now—back to the story.

We took a little detour to lay out the real estate playbook, but life? Life doesn't follow bullet points.

And while I was out there selling homes and stacking wins, something underneath was starting to crack.

Because success is loud, but emptiness whispers.

And I was about to hear both, clear as day.

Chapter 12

Breaking Before the Breakthrough

Rock bottom doesn't always look like disaster. Sometimes it looks like success. Clean clothes. Big checks. Applause. A full calendar and an empty soul.

That was me.

From the outside, everything looked golden. The deals were closing. The phone was ringing. I had momentum, status, options. People thought I was thriving.

But inside? I was cracking.

Not all at once. Piece by piece. Compromise by compromise. I had spent years chasing highs, attention, and anything that could numb the quiet. And I'd gotten good at it—so good that I almost believed it myself.

Almost.

Because the truth was, I wasn't just tired—I was hollow. I didn't want more money. I didn't want another party. I didn't want another fling. I wanted to feel something real. I wanted peace—the kind that doesn't disappear when the music stops or the inbox fills up. I wanted to wake up without regret gnawing at my gut.

I used to think happiness came with success. That if I just earned enough, proved enough, looked good enough—I'd finally feel it.

But the more I won, the worse it got.

And then it hit me: If I kept living like this, my life would end up as a highlight reel of moments that looked great from a distance but didn't feel like mine up close. A carefully edited montage of wins, smiles, and just enough vulnerability to seem authentic. I wasn't building a life—I was building a brochure. And honestly? Even the brochure was starting to feel like false advertising.

And the truth was, I wasn't okay.

I had everything a person needs to make something good of their life—a decent body, a sharp mind, and parents who actually cared. And still, I used all of it to chase the next rush, the next escape, the next temporary fix.

I had sex before I could spell it. I was looking at porn before kindergarten. And by my twenties, I was addicted to more than just drugs. I hadn't just made a few bad choices—I had trained myself to live in the darkness. The truth is, I didn't ease into addiction. I dove in headfirst. I was always fast. Fast to act. Fast to perform. Fast to overdo it. While my friends were experimenting, I was already neck deep. What they tried in moderation, I consumed in extremes. One friend here, another there— each one dabbling while I was quietly outpacing them all. I wasn't chasing trouble for fun. I was chasing it because I didn't know how to stop.

Losing Lia hurt—but it wasn't just the heartbreak. It was the realization that the fantasy I'd built in my head wasn't going to save me. I'd convinced myself that marriage would fix everything. That love would be my redemption arc. That if I could just build a life with someone, the rest would sort itself out. But when she left, it wasn't just her I lost. I lost the illusion. The idea that some external solution would heal what was broken inside me. No wedding, no woman, no success was going to change the truth I didn't want to face: I had to deal with my life. I had to deal with me.

And once that illusion was gone, the noise got louder. The distractions didn't work like they used to. The parties felt emptier. The money felt smaller. The grind lost its edge. Everything I'd built to keep myself numb started to crack. I was still showing up, still making moves, still stacking wins—but underneath, I was unraveling. Quietly. Invisibly. The hollowness had become so normal, I started mistaking it for peace. I could still laugh on cue, light up a room, post the wins—but it was all just polish on something quietly falling apart. But when it got quiet— when the lights went off and the phone stopped buzzing—I couldn't outrun it. That ache. That pit. That voice asking, *Is this really it?*

And that question—Is this really it?—started showing up everywhere. In the car. In the shower. In the silence between songs. It was never loud, but it was relentless. It was in the eyes of strangers. In the empty bed after a night out. In the mirror, when I barely recognized the guy staring back. I had everything they said would make me happy—and yet I was more miserable than I'd ever been. That's when I realized: The hustle wasn't healing me. It was hiding me. I wasn't building a life—I was building a fortress. One success at a time. One dollar. One deal. One distraction. But no matter how high I stacked the walls, the pain always found its way in. And slowly, I started to see the truth I didn't want to face:

I wasn't in control.

Not of the highs. Not of the lows. Not of anything in-between.

The Quiet Pursuit

Here's a detail that might surprise you: The first time I ever really read scripture—like *actually* sat down and opened the pages with my full attention—I was high.

Not during some profound, sober search for meaning. I wasn't kneeling beside a bed or crying out in desperation. I was just stoned. Bored. And for once, my brain wasn't bouncing off the walls.

I'd gone up to Chandler, AZ, to clean out a house I was trying to sell. I had left a few boxes behind in the vacant property, and at some point during a showing, someone had rifled through them and stolen from me. I didn't even know anything was missing until I got a call from the Secret Service telling me my passport and personal checks were being duplicated and handed out.

So I drove up to get everything sorted. It wasn't a great day.

As I was digging through the mess, trying to salvage what was left, I found something I hadn't seen in years: a set of scriptures someone had given me when I was eight years old. Dusty. Forgotten. Just sitting there in the box like they'd been waiting for me.

And for some reason—I don't know why—I picked them up, opened the cover, started reading.

No glowing screen. No remote. Just silence, pages, and whatever chemicals were still pumping through my system.

But here's the crazy part: Something got through.

The words didn't hit like lightning or wrap me in a holy glow. But they *hit*. Somewhere in the haze and stillness, they started working on me. Not in a loud way. Not in a way I could explain. But something ancient, something true, was waking up inside me.

The Power of a Praying Mother

Then there was my mom. We never talked about any of it. We didn't need to.

Because I could feel her prayers—like they had mass, like they carried weight. They weren't just words whispered into the ceiling. They had gravity. They pressed against my chest every time I tried to slip back into numbness. Like some invisible tether pulling me back when I drifted too far.

She didn't preach. She didn't push. She just prayed. Quietly. Faithfully.

And somehow . . . I felt it.

And maybe that's why, even when everything around me started falling apart, I didn't completely fall with it. Because her prayers were like an anchor—subtle, but steady. They didn't stop the storm. But they reminded me I had somewhere to come back to.

And I hated it.

I hated the way it made me feel. I hated that she wouldn't just give up on me. I hated that deep down, I knew she was right.

But I never told her any of that.

And if she ever reads this book, this will be the first time she knows.

When "Real" Finally Hit

Even after I started reading scripture—high or not—I still didn't know what to do with the weight of my life.

I believed God was real. I had felt Him. But knowing He was real didn't erase the mess I had made.

So I carried it.

For weeks, I walked around with the full weight of everything I'd done. All the moments I had justified. All the choices I had brushed off. The girls. The manipulation. The drinking. The masks. The pride. All of it.

And I started thinking about a verse I hadn't even known was in there until I read it:

"Come unto me, all ye that labour and are heavy laden, and I will give you rest."

I had been laboring.

And I was heavy laden.

But rest? That felt like something I didn't deserve. I wasn't a guy who got *rest*. I was the guy who earned what he got. And by this point, I knew what I had earned.

So finally, one night, after weeks of walking around with that weight, I did the only thing that made sense.

I knelt down to pray.

It had been years since I'd actually knelt and talked to God. But one night, with nothing left to lose, I got down on my knees. And I stayed there.

I poured it all out. The drugs. The drinking. The girls. The pride. The lies. The hurt I'd caused. It was a full-blown, soul-wrenching confession—me naming every sin I could remember and begging God to somehow still want me.

I didn't feel better as I went.

I felt worse.

The deeper I dug, the heavier it got.

Every time I thought, *That had to be the worst of it*, another memory surfaced. Another choice I had buried. Another moment I had shoved down so deep I forgot it still had a grip on me.

The prayer kept going. Not a neat little checklist. Not a polished sermon. It was messy. Painful. Unfiltered.

It was me, face down on the floor, whispering out my regrets like I was trying to vomit up the past.

And the wild part? I *wanted* to feel worse.

Somehow, I thought if I just punished myself enough—if I sat in it long enough—I could prove I was sorry. I could earn my way back into grace. But the more I talked, the more the shame piled on. And the heavier it got, the more convinced I became that this was how it would end.

This was my payment.

This was the price.

There was no magic switch, no sudden warmth, no whisper from heaven that made it better.

Just silence. Weight. And the haunting thought, *Maybe this is what I deserve.*

I don't know how long it went on—five hours? Six? I lost track of time.

But then, in the middle of it all—mid-confession, mid-tear, mid-*I'll never be enough*—it happened.

Something lifted.

It wasn't dramatic at first. It didn't feel like a snap or a jolt. Just a lightness. A slow untying of the knots in my chest. Like someone had been pulling on the rope wrapped around my heart—and finally, they let go.

And then?

It was gone.

All of it.

The guilt. The shame. The heaviness. The voice in my head that had told me for years, *You're too far gone. You'll never be clean. This is just who you are.*

Silenced.

The ache in my chest? Gone.

Self-hatred? Gone.

The weight I didn't even realize I'd been carrying since I was a child?

Lifted.

And it was replaced with something I hadn't felt in years—maybe ever.

Peace.

Like I could finally take a full breath without choking on regret.

All of it. The guilt. The shame. The heaviness. All gone.

At first, I panicked.

Where did it go?

Why don't I feel anything?

I almost missed the misery—because I'd gotten used to it. But in its place came something I didn't expect:

Peace.

Not the "I think I feel better" kind. The real thing.

And then I heard it—not audibly, but clearly: *You're forgiven. I've taken this from you.*

Now, if this had been a movie, I'd have smiled and whispered, "Thank you." But no—this was me, the guy who questioned everything. So I shot back, "Sure. That's probably just my brain trying to cope."

And then I heard it again—more direct this time: *No. I am more than that. I have the power to forgive you.*

And what did I say?

"Prove it."

Yes, I really said that. Childlike, dumb, bold—I don't know. But I said it.

And God answered.

What happened next?

I will never be able to fully explain it.

I felt something move through me. Light. Pure light. Like joy itself had become tangible and was being poured into my chest. And it didn't stop.

It kept coming—filling me, flooding me. I felt warm. Weightless. Free. So full of peace and joy that it almost scared me.

It felt like I was being hugged from the inside out. Like every dark place in my body was being flushed clean.

And it kept building—until it was almost too much.

I remember literally saying out loud, **"Okay! I get it! Please stop; I know you are here!"** because it felt like I might explode from the intensity of it all.

And that's when I knew.

It wasn't me. It wasn't my brain. It wasn't some emotional placebo. **It was Him.**

Born Again

There's a phrase in scripture that says, *Born again.*

I used to think that sounded dramatic. Like, okay, sure, you prayed and now you're "born again." Cool story, church guy.

But now?

Now I get it.

Because that night felt like a death and a birth.

The version of me that had spent his whole life pretending to be fine had died. The one who wore success like armor and shame like perfume—just enough to cover the stench.

I was born into something else.

Something freer.

Something lighter.

But looking back, I can say this with full honesty: **Freedom isn't the same as ease.**

Yes—He forgave me. He took the weight. He set me free from the punishment and the shame of everything I had done.

But I still carry the scars.

The addictions didn't vanish like smoke—they just lost their control. I still wake up every day aware of how close I am to falling right back into it. One drink. One party. One slip. That life is always just *one decision* away.

And I pray—every single day—that He keeps me strong enough not to go back.

Because I know what's waiting for me on the other side of that choice. And I know that without Him, I'd already be there.

So no—freedom doesn't mean I never struggle.

It means I *finally* know who to lean on when I do.

That makes all the difference.

Walking Away, Then Coming Back

After that night—after the weight lifted, after the light poured in—I knew something had to change.

But not everything changed overnight.

I still had the same friends. The same places. The same rhythms. And while I loved them dearly, I started to realize something uncomfortable: I wasn't strong enough to live a new life while standing in the middle of my old one.

It wasn't because they were bad people. Far from it. These were some of the best friends I'd ever had—ride-or-die, laugh-until-you-can't-breathe, show-up-at-three-a.m. kind of friends. But the life we'd built together? It revolved around things I was trying to leave behind.

So, I made one of the hardest decisions of my life.

I stepped away.

Quietly. Gently. Without drama or judgment. I told them, "I love you guys. I'll be back. But right now, I've got to figure out who I am without all this noise."

And they respected it.

They didn't understand it at the time—but they gave me space. And that space? It saved me.

Because as much as I missed them, I needed a season where it was just me and God. No distractions. No temptations. Just quiet growth.

And eventually, I came back.

Not all at once, and not as the same person. I wasn't perfect. I wasn't finished. But I was different—more grounded, more centered, more *me* than I'd ever been.

And the most beautiful part?

They were still there. Still cheering me on. Still willing to walk with me.

Turns out, I didn't have to lose them to find myself.

And that? That's the kind of redemption I'll never stop being grateful for.

I had no idea what was coming next. But now, for the first time, I wasn't chasing it alone.

Chapter 13

Romance, Regret, and Really Bad Timing

The next few chapters? They're not about business. They're not about sales. They're not about flipping houses, building trade schools, or making payroll by sheer force of will.

They're about *her.*

Candice.

The girl who wrecked my focus, reordered my priorities, and showed me a kind of love I didn't know existed—and also made me feel like a total idiot more times than I'd care to admit.

You might've grabbed this book for the business lessons—and they're here—but you need to know this: I hustled long before Candice. The difference is, back then I was hustling for the wrong reasons. I was trying to impress, to prove, to attract someone like her. But when she actually showed up? That's when I realized hustle isn't about chasing attention—it's about building something real, something worth keeping. Candice didn't start my grind, but she turned it into purpose.

But if you've ever fallen for someone you weren't sure would fall back . . .

If you've ever chased something that didn't make sense on paper, but made perfect sense to your heart . . .

If you've ever thought, *I might be totally screwed here, but I have to try . . .*

Then keep reading.

This part's not just love story. It's the turning point.

The First Dance and a Twist of Fate

The right woman doesn't just inspire a man—she reorients his entire universe.

She becomes the gravity he builds around.

The reason he pushes past pain, sharpens his tools, and keeps showing up.

We'll say we're building for legacy, for wealth, for pride—but the truth?

We're chasing her light.

And when she shines on us—even for a second—we'll build higher than we ever thought we could, just to stay in her orbit.

Because the only way God could improve on man, was to give him a woman.

Not to complete him—but to awaken what strength alone never could.

She's not just part of our world.

She's the star we were spinning toward all along.

The hardest negotiation, the most intense pursuit, the deal that took every ounce of effort?

That was her.

And I was about to put it all on the line.

I had a knack for getting people to move. If someone could keep a basic rhythm, I could teach them to dance. Confidence? I could fake that for them. Coordination? That was a little trickier—but if they held on tight and trusted me, we could usually make it work.

That's why when she walked into my class for the first time, I wasn't worried about whether she could follow my steps—I was more interested in the effortless charm she carried.

She was new to dancing—her first time on a real ballroom floor. But she was just so darn cute and flirty, it didn't matter.

She could keep the rhythm with her feet, and honestly, that's all it takes to make someone *look* like they've been dancing for years.

The rest? I could teach. But that kind of charm? That walks in on its own.

I don't remember what we talked about as we danced, but I do remember how easy it was. She wasn't nervous, awkward, or hesitant like most beginners. She was confident, playful, and—without even trying—completely captivating.

After the lesson, as was tradition, I invited everyone back to my place to hang out. She showed up. The flirting continued. It wasn't forced or over the top—it was just natural. Like we had known each other forever.

Then came the moment that nearly made me fall out of my chair.

A friend leaned over and muttered, "Dude . . . She's seventeen."

I froze.

No. No way. That couldn't be right.

She seemed far too mature for seventeen. I had dated women in their thirties who didn't have the level of confidence, self-assurance, and presence that she had. I laughed it off at first, but then the reality set in.

I had been openly flirting with a seventeen-year-old all night, as a twenty-two-year-old.

Abort mission. Retreat. Fall back.

I immediately took a step back—not physically, but mentally. It wasn't like I had been planning anything inappropriate—I was done with those days—but the age gap? That was a problem.

At least, that's what I thought.

The next morning, I walked into church, because the new Clay would never miss a day of church. There she was—standing at the pulpit, delivering a talk.

Now, this was strange for one big reason—this was a single adult ward. You had to have graduated from high school to be there.

She hadn't graduated.

So why was she up there, speaking like she belonged?

I sat in my seat, stunned. Not just because she was there, but because she was good. She spoke with warmth and confidence, like someone who had been doing this for years.

And then her dad got up to speak.

And suddenly, everything made sense.

Her dad was the High Councilman in our ward—essentially one of the church leaders who helped oversee things. I had met him before, but at that moment, something clicked.

I suddenly remembered a conversation I'd had months earlier with my friend James.

James had gone on a date with the high councilman's daughter, a girl who he swore was the most beautiful girl he had ever seen. He was completely smitten. But after one date, she told him he was too old for her.

At the time, I had laughed it off and never thought about it again.

Until now.

I looked at her. Then at her dad.

No way.

James had been talking about her.

And now, here she was.

In my dance class.

At my house.

Standing at the pulpit of my church.

And just when I thought this situation couldn't get any more ridiculous, her dad started telling a story—about how he met his wife.

He had just returned from his mission at twenty-one years old when he met a beautiful girl who was still in high school.

Not only that, but he had even taken her to her senior prom before they got married.

I nearly choked.

Well. There it is. The answer to all my concerns.

If her dad had been in the exact same situation, how could he possibly be upset if I asked his daughter out?

And just like that, bad timing didn't seem like such a bad excuse anymore.

So, after church, I found her walking out to her car and made my move.

I walked up beside her and, trying to sound casual, said,

"I know I'm an old man, but would you be willing to let me take you on a date?"

She didn't hesitate.

"Yes."

And just like that, I got my first date.

Those first few months? Perfect.

We didn't just date—we thrived. Everything about our relationship felt effortless. We laughed, we danced, we had long conversations that felt like they could stretch on forever.

Candice fit into my life like she had always been there.

And that scared me.

I had never been in a relationship where I wasn't worried about how much the other person cared. There was no chasing, no proving myself, no wondering if I was enough. Candice never said she loved me, but I could see it in the way she looked at me, hear it in the way she spoke to me, feel it in the way I had somehow become her top priority.

And that made me uneasy.

Because if she was willing to marry me—and I knew she was— then how could she be sure I was the right choice? She was so young.

How could she possibly know I was worth choosing for the rest of her life if she had never even looked at what else was out there?

Then she told me she was going off to college in Idaho.

To any sane person, this wouldn't have been a problem. People do long-distance all the time.

But in my twenty-two-year-old mind?

Long-distance = bad idea.

I had been through that before, and I had no interest in doing it again.

So instead of figuring out a way to make it work, I sat Candice down and delivered one of the dumbest breakup speeches in human history.

"You should date around while you're in college. You know, make sure I'm the right guy. See what else is out there. If you don't find anyone better, then you'll know I was the right choice all along."

Now, let's pause here for a second.

If I had any sense, I would have realized I was essentially handing Candice a permission slip to replace me. Instead, in my head, this was somehow the noble thing to do. I was giving her freedom! I was letting her explore!

I was also a complete idiot.

Because the only problem?

Candice didn't want to break up.

She fought it.

She didn't understand why I was throwing something so good away.

She told me she was willing to do long-distance, that she was willing to make it work, that she didn't want anyone else.

And I still broke up with her.

The Other Excuse I Used (That I Shouldn't Have)

Now, I'd love to tell you that was the only reason I broke up with Candice.

But there was one more thing that tipped the scales in my mind.

Right around the time I was debating the breakup, I had been set apart for a church calling, and one of the counselors in the bishopric decided it was the perfect moment to pronounce an extra blessing on me.

Which was fine. Except for one tiny issue.

He decided to tell me I wouldn't get married in the temple—that I would marry a nonmember instead.

Now, to be clear, this guy did not have the right or the authority to say this. But for whatever reason, it got in my head. I had already been wondering if I should break up with Candice, and suddenly, I had confirmation that maybe I was supposed to.

Candice did not take this well.

She immediately told me, in no uncertain terms, that this guy was completely wrong, a giant idiot.

And she was right.

She tried so hard to convince me that this wasn't a good reason to throw us away.

But the truth?

I had already made up my mind.

I had never dated someone like Candice before, and I guess part of me thought maybe I should.

Maybe I should date more girls like her—just to make sure she really was the one too.

Candice, to her credit, did not go down without a fight.

She was hurt. Betrayed. She didn't understand why I couldn't just trust what we had.

But she was fighting against a guy who had already decided.

And I was stubborn.

The Breakup That Wasn't Exactly a Breakup

We still saw each other a few times before she left.

And even though we had officially ended things, we still kissed.

More than once.

Now, let's be clear. We weren't trying to backtrack on the breakup. But at the same time, we weren't exactly acting like exes, either.

Each time it happened, there was that lingering moment afterward—where we both seemed to ask the same silent question:

Are we really doing this? Are we really walking away from something this good?

But I was stubborn.

No matter how much I cared about her, I told myself it was for the best. She needed to experience college. She needed to date other guys. And—if she still wanted me after all of that—then maybe, just maybe, we'd find our way back to each other.

But even before she left, there was one guy who made me wonder if I had made a mistake.

The Air Force Pilot

This guy was as good-looking as they come, had his life completely together, and—to top it off—was literally a fighter pilot. You know, the type of guy women swoon over in movies? That guy.

And Candice was dating him.

At that point, I figured this was it. Candice was getting a preview of what else was out there, and if I'm being honest, I figured this was the guy who would officially replace me.

Then, she went to visit him.

And when she came back?

She kissed me.

And then said, "I can't stand him."

I couldn't believe it. Not because she kissed me—I kind of expected that.

But because she had dated the guy I thought was the ultimate catch and still ended up back here. It messed with me.

For the first time, I wondered . . .

What if she really doesn't find anyone better?

Still, I told myself it was for the best.

Then she moved to Idaho.

I figured that was the end.

She dated. I dated.

Story over.

Chapter 14

The Dance That Changed Everything

Two years had passed since Candice and I broke up. Two years since I had convinced myself I had made the right decision. And in those two years, I did everything I thought I was supposed to do.

I dated other girls. I kept busy. I moved forward.

And yet, sitting in church that Sunday morning, nothing could have prepared me for what happened next.

Candice walked in.

And suddenly, I forgot everything else.

Up until five seconds ago, I was feeling pretty great about my life. I was sitting next to my girlfriend—a drop-dead gorgeous Puerto Rican bombshell, who was as kind as she was stunning.

She had been nothing but good to me. There was no reason for me to feel like anything was missing. Until Candice walked through the door.

Time stopped.

She was even more beautiful than I remembered, and it hit me like a freight train.

That was my girl.

Suddenly, everything I had convinced myself over the past two years felt wrong. I had told myself that breaking up was smart. But at that exact moment, all I could think was this:

I really, really hope she didn't find someone better.

I needed to talk to Candice. I managed to get one conversation in with her that week. It was short—friendly, but distant. She mentioned she was going to a Friday night church dance. That was all I needed to hear. That was my territory. I had to be there.

I had to make sure Candice noticed me. I also had to make sure I was single. And that meant immediately breaking up with my girlfriend. Which I did. That same day.

And she did not take it well.

But in my mind, it was simple: I was either going to marry Candice, or I was going to have to watch someone else do it.

And I was not about to let that happen. I couldn't risk showing up to that dance with a girlfriend while the love of my life was right there in front of me.

Friday night arrived, and I walked into the dance feeling determined. Candice was already there.

This time, we mostly danced together. Sure, we threw in a few swing dances, switching things up here and there, but for the most part, it was just us.

It wasn't just casual partners rotating in and out. It was intentional. Focused. There was a rhythm between us that hadn't faded at all. She was intrigued. She was enjoying it.

And when I asked, "Hey, you want to grab some dessert after this?" She agreed. Immediately.

The Dessert That Felt Like Old Times

As we left the dance, I was feeling really good about how the night was going. Then, as we were driving to get dessert, Candice crashed her dad's truck into another car while she was parking. I was standing there and watched the whole scene play out in slow motion.

Now, most people might take this as a bad omen. A sign that the night was about to go terribly wrong. Not me.

If anything, I took it as a sign from the universe that things were about to get interesting. Luckily, it wasn't a serious accident—just a minor bump—but I could tell Candice was mortified.

She got out, handled the situation like a pro, and then we went to get dessert anyway.

And that's when it happened.

As we sat across from each other, laughing, talking, and eating, it felt like nothing had changed.

Like no time had passed.

Like the breakup had never happened.

We were us again.

For the first time in two years, I really thought,

Maybe this is just going to fall back into place. Maybe she still feels the same way I do.

I left that night completely convinced that things were back on track.

I had no idea how wrong I was.

In my mind, we had just reconnected.

In Candice's mind?

Not so fast.

The next month was filled with silence.

I called—no answer.

I waited—no call back.

The Cold Reality Check

I started to realize something: Just because *I* had made up my mind didn't mean Candice had made up *hers.*

For two years, I'd been in the driver's seat. I was the one who broke up with her. I was the one who thought I had it all figured out. I was the one who believed I could just waltz back into her life like, *Hey, remember me? Good news—I'm ready now!*

Now?

She was in control.

And I was stuck waiting in the emotional DMV, hoping my number would get called.

About a month went by. Memorial Day weekend was coming up, and honestly, I was starting to lose hope. We talked a few times here and there, but it felt like leaving voicemails for a celebrity hotline—short, one-sided, and you know they're never calling back—awkward, short, and kind of humiliating.

Still, I managed to get her to promise me a date the next time she came down to visit her family. And I knew that visit was happening. I had the weekend marked on my calendar with a red Sharpie, like it was the Second Coming.

Friday came. I called her.

No answer.

Saturday came and went. Still nothing. Not even a "hey, can't talk right now" text. At this point, I was half convinced she'd changed her number and left the country.

Then Sunday hit. And that day . . . Oh, that day lasted a decade.

I paced. I prayed. I checked my phone so many times I'm pretty sure I gave myself thumb arthritis. I even cleaned my whole house—which should tell you how emotionally unstable I was.

By Sunday night, I had convinced myself she was never going to call. That she had met someone new. Probably someone with a real job. Probably someone who didn't have a history of clowning, balloon animals, and multiple near-death business ventures.

She was supposed to leave on Tuesday morning.

And now it was Monday.

Memorial Day.

The last possible day.

And I didn't have a plan.

All I had was a stomach full of dread, a brain full of overanalyzing, and a phone that might as well have been a brick for how useless it had been all weekend.

It wasn't just the silence that got me—it was the *not knowing*. Was she still deciding? Was she already decided? Was she ghosting me out of kindness or confusion?

And the worst part? I couldn't blame her.

I mean, look at the résumé: emotionally unpredictable, wildly ambitious, known to run at the first sign of peace and stability. Sure, I had changed. Sure, I was trying. But from her side of the fence, I probably still looked like a guy holding a bouquet of red flags.

But none of that mattered.

Because I still wanted a shot.

Even if I had to wait until the very last minute.

A Conversation with the Unseen

So there I was.

Memorial Day morning. No call. No text. No hope.

I'd tried everything. Left messages. Said prayers. Pitched my case to God more times than I could count. And still—nothing. Just silence and the slow, creeping certainty that she was gone for good.

That's when a memory floated back into my head.

Every Memorial Day growing up, my family would visit the cemetery to honor my older brother—the one who was stillborn. It was a quiet tradition. One of those sacred, subtle things that shaped my childhood without ever being explained. We didn't talk about it much. But we went. Almost every year.

And now, for the first time in a long time, it felt like that's exactly where I needed to be.

I didn't really understand why. It just felt right. Like some unseen hand was nudging me toward something I couldn't see yet, and hey, I really needed something to take my mind off Candice.

So I got in the car and drove.

I pulled into the cemetery lot under that dry Arizona sky, the kind that makes even silence feel louder. I turned off the engine. Rolled the window down. And just sat there. It was quiet. The kind of quiet that presses on your chest and makes you suddenly aware of every thought you've been trying to outrun.

I wasn't there to have a moment. I wasn't praying. Honestly, I just needed a break from pacing around like a lovesick teenager. But then— clear as a bell—I heard it.

"Thanks for coming to visit me today."

I froze.

Nobody was there. I hadn't said a word out loud. But something inside me knew—I wasn't alone anymore.

I didn't hear a voice like thunder. It wasn't a booming proclamation from the clouds. It was quieter than that. More personal. Like a memory, but more alive. Like someone had slipped into the room of my soul without opening the door.

"It's nice to be here," I heard myself say, the words tumbling out of my mouth before my brain had a chance to filter them.

And just like that, I wasn't grieving alone anymore.

"So . . . How are things?" he asked, gently.

I let out a laugh—half chuckle, half exhaustion.

"Not great."

And then I started walking.

I didn't even think about where I was going. I just knew. My feet carried me down that old familiar path until I saw it—my brother's grave.

And right next to it? A bench. Old. Worn. Still sturdy.

It must've been placed there by my family more than twenty years ago. And somehow, it was still standing. Waiting.

So I sat down.

And I started talking.

About Candice. About the years we'd been apart. About the hope I'd built up and the wall she kept rebuilding. About the way I wanted so badly for it to work but felt powerless to make it happen.

I told him everything. Like he was an old friend. Like we'd done this before.

And somewhere in the middle of my venting, I let slip the line I hadn't said out loud to anyone—not even myself.

"I don't deserve her anyway."

"Why do you think that?" he asked.

I hesitated.

"Because I am not a good person."

I swallowed hard.

"I mean . . . I've changed. I've tried. I've turned my life around. But the stuff I've done? It's still in me. I struggle every day. And no matter how hard I try, it just never feels like enough."

I expected silence. Or maybe some kind of cosmic shrug.

But instead . . . he laughed.

"Clay . . . Do you really think that's how this works?"

I blinked. "I don't know. Maybe?"

"You're not perfect. You're not supposed to be. But you're trying. And that means something. You're worth more than you give yourself credit for."

I closed my eyes.

And for the first time in a long time—I actually believed it.

And then he said something that shook me to my core.

"I'm glad you made it today. We agreed to meet here, remember?"

"Uh, what do you mean?"

"Before we came to Earth. You and I made this deal, to meet here—on my birthday."

My breath caught in my throat.

The moment he said it, I looked down—and my heart stopped.

His birthdate. His death date.

This wasn't just any day.

I had unknowingly come to visit my brother on the exact day he was born and died.

Tears welled in my eyes, and in that instant, I completely lost control.

I was sitting at his grave, talking out loud to someone no one else could see, sobbing so hard that if anyone walked by, they would think I had lost my mind.

"Why?" I finally managed. "Why did you have to die?"

"Because we both couldn't come. One of us had to stay behind."

I clenched my fists, swallowing the lump in my throat.

"If I had lived," he continued, **"Mom wouldn't have had you."**

I let out a breath, my whole body trembling.

It hit me like a tidal wave—I had found out that my Savior had died for me, and now I was realizing that more had been given to me.

I had two brothers who had given their lives so that I could be here.

One who died for my soul.

And one who stayed behind so I could take his place.

And in that moment, it all clicked.

I wasn't a mistake.

I wasn't a burden.

I wasn't some guy clawing through life trying to prove he was enough.

I was meant to be here.

I had been chosen—twice.

I looked at his grave, blinking back tears.

"So . . . What do I do . . . What do I do about Candice?"

His voice came softly, like it had the whole time.

"Call Candice. Exactly at noon."

I laughed through my sniffles. "That's it?"

"That's it. She'll pick up. And everything will be fine."

There was a pause.

And then he said, almost like a smile was in his voice,

"I gotta go. You're going to be fine. And we'll see each other again."

Then he was gone.

No fade-out. No slow goodbye. Just . . . gone.

And I felt it immediately.

The second he left, the air shifted. The bench felt colder. The stillness grew heavier.

The whole time he'd been there, I kept thinking,

This is probably just me. I'm being weird. I'm talking to the spirit of my dead brother like it's normal.

But when he left?

I knew.

It had been real.

Because the silence that followed didn't just feel empty—it felt like something *had* been there, and now it wasn't.

I sat with that for a moment. Let it sink in.

Then I looked at the time.

10:30 a.m.

I had an hour and a half until noon.

So I did the only thing that made sense.

I stayed.

I trimmed the desert brush around his headstone. Cleared the dust from the lettering. Pulled up the scraggly weeds growing at the base. Not because it needed to be perfect—but because I needed it to be.

If we had really made that deal before either of us was born, then I was going to show up for it—fully.

When I finished, I sat back on that old bench—tired, quiet, more grounded than I'd felt in years.

I took a breath that filled every corner of my lungs. And I waited.

The Moment of Truth

11:59 a.m.

Deep breath.

12:00 p.m. exactly.

I dialed.

And she picked up.

No hesitation. No ignoring me. No letting it go to voicemail.

Just— "Oh, hey."

Like she had been expecting my call. Like it was totally normal that she had ghosted me for the entire weekend.

I tried to play it cool, even though my heart was racing.

"Hey, how's it going?"

"Good," she said, sounding casual. Too casual.

I tried not to overanalyze her tone.

I asked her about her weekend, about her family. I waited for her to bring up our date that never happened.

She never did.

So finally, I went for it.

"So . . . I thought we were gonna go out this weekend?"

A pause.

"Oh," she said, like she had just remembered. "Yeah, sorry. I got busy."

That was it.

That was the excuse.

She had gotten busy.

I knew I was losing ground, so I pivoted to the next-best move.

"Okay, well, how about I take you out tonight before you head back?"

Another pause.

"Oh, I can't—I have plans with my family."

And just like that, it was slipping away again.

I opened my mouth to push one last time—and then it happened.

Candice's mom entered the chat.

"Who's that?"

Candice hesitated.

"It's Clay."

Her mom, without missing a beat: "Oh, Clay! Invite him over for dinner!"

I could hear Candice start to protest—

But I was not about to let her get a word in.

I seized the moment.

"Sounds great! I'll be there."

And then—I hung up.

Before she could change her mind. Before she could backtrack.

Before she could say anything that might undo this miracle of an invitation.

I sat there, staring at my phone, barely able to believe what had just happened.

Somehow, against all odds, I had just gotten an invitation to her family's house—directly from her mom.

Candice's Reaction at the Memorial Day Barbecue

What kind of grown man writes a six-page love letter?

Apparently, I do.

It wasn't a normal thing for me. I wasn't the kind of guy to sit down and pour my feelings onto paper. Now, based on the stories about girls I am telling in this book, it might not seem like it, but I had always been the type who, if a girl didn't like me, I'd shrug it off and move on. No big deal. There were plenty of other girls in the world.

But Candice?

Candice was different.

I don't know when it happened, but at some point between breaking up with her and watching her walk back into my life, she had become the one girl I couldn't get out of my head.

And I hated that.

I hated that she had this much control over me.

I hated that no matter how much I tried to let her go, I couldn't.

I hated that I was sitting in my car, about to walk into her parents' house for dinner—clutching a six-page love letter I had written like this was a totally normal thing to do.

This wasn't me. She had me in a chokehold.

Looking back, the love letter was an absolutely ridiculous idea. But at the time? It felt like my only idea.

Here's the logic my desperate, lovesick brain had come up with:

Candice clearly wasn't into talking to me.

When she did talk to me, the conversations were brief, surface level, and distant.

If I actually saw her in person, she'd probably avoid me like the plague.

But if I wrote everything down—every feeling, every thought, every reason I still wanted to be with her—she would finally understand.

And if she understood, maybe she'd love me again.

Of course, none of this was a well-thought-out plan.

It was panic-mode romance.

A last-ditch Hail Mary.

It was me grasping at the absolute last straw, convinced that if I just found the right words, she would stop running from me.

So, I sat down and wrote. Six full pages, front and back.

I don't even remember everything I said. Something about how I had been an idiot. How I had never stopped thinking about her. How I wanted her to at least consider giving me another chance.

The entire time, I knew this was crazy.

But I couldn't stop myself.

And once it was done, I did the worst possible thing.

I brought it with me.

Because nothing says "I'm totally a sane and well-adjusted human being" like showing up at your ex's family barbecue, carrying a handwritten, six-page, front-and-back emotional manifesto.

The Coldest Welcome Ever

From the moment I walked into Candice's house, I could feel it.

She did not want me there.

Her entire vibe screamed, *Why are you in my house?*

Meanwhile, her family?

Her mom was all smiles.

Her dad shook my hand like I was his new best friend.

Her sister, who I had never even met before, greeted me warmly.

Candice, though?

Nothing.

She avoided eye contact. She dodged me at every turn.

I tried to sit near her—she got up and moved.

I tried to help in the kitchen—suddenly, she had something else to do.

I walked outside to get some fresh air—she went inside.

She was treating me like I was some random door-to-door salesman who wouldn't take the hint.

Which, to be fair, maybe I was.

So, at this point, I had two choices:

1. Be a normal, self-respecting human being, realize she's over it, and leave.

2. Double down on my stupidity and give her the letter anyway.

Of course, I chose option two.

But not yet.

I had to play this smart.

So instead of following her around like some lost puppy, I pivoted. I turned on the charm full blast—with her family.

Basically, I was winning over everyone in the room except the one person I was actually there for.

But I wasn't just doing this for fun. I was waiting.

Waiting for my moment.

Dinner came and went, and the night dragged on. Candice stayed busy, always finding something to do, somewhere else to be. It was getting late, and I knew my window was closing.

Finally, after hours of being ignored, I just went for it.

I walked up to her and said, "Hey, can you walk me out?"

She hesitated.

And in that moment, I saw hope.

Then, to my absolute shock, she said,

"Sure."

The Love Letter Moment—Her Immediate Reaction

I walked out of Candice's house, the letter burning a hole in my back pocket.

Every step toward my car felt heavier, like I was dragging the last shred of my dignity behind me.

I had no idea if I was going to go through with it.

I had been playing this moment over and over in my head for days.

We walked toward my car together, the night air thick with awkwardness.

Candice kept a careful distance, her arms crossed, her expression unreadable.

When we reached my car, I pulled out my keys and opened the door, fully prepared to leave.

This was the moment of no return.

If I got in, I was accepting defeat.

If I didn't . . . well, I was about to make a complete fool of myself.

My fingers tightened on the door handle.

Then, I turned to her.

My heart was pounding. My mouth was dry.

"I have something for you."

She raised an eyebrow, clearly not interested in whatever I was about to say.

I reached into my back pocket and pulled out the letter—carefully folded into a heart, because apparently, I had the emotional intelligence of a nine-year-old girl at a slumber party.

Candice stared at it.

Then, hesitantly, she reached out and took it.

I could see it already. She was going to glance at it, force a polite thank-you, then throw it away the second I drove off.

I couldn't let that happen.

Before she could even look at the first word, I panicked.

"Actually . . . Can I just read it to you?"

Her head snapped up.

She blinked—clearly surprised.

And honestly? So was I.

Because here's the thing: This was a *terrible* idea. I've never been a great reader. I didn't even finish my first real book until I was out of high school and selling Cutco knives. I'm not kidding. I avoided reading growing up like it was the dentist. I'd scan a few lines, guess the rest, and pray no one called on me in class.

So now here I was—offering to read *my own writing* out loud, to the girl I'd spent years hoping to win back.

Flawless plan, right?

It was like challenging Michael Jordan to a dunk contest, knowing full well you just learned how to tie your shoes.

But something in me knew I couldn't let her read it on her own. Not yet. I needed her to *hear* it—mistakes, stumbles, awkward pauses and all. Because as much as I wanted the words to be perfect . . . I knew they mattered more if they came from me.

This wasn't about punctuation.

It was about heart.

And my heart had a lot to say.

"You want to read it to me?"

I nodded, suddenly realizing how insane this was.

But I had come too far.

She shrugged. "Sure."

I took a deep breath.

And I read every single word.

I didn't look up.

I didn't check her expression.

I just kept reading, my voice shaking, my heart hammering.

Page one.

Page two.

Page three.

Still, I kept my eyes glued to the paper, refusing to see how she was reacting.

Page four.

Page five.

Page six.

By the time I finished, my throat was dry, and my hands were shaking.

I finally looked up.

Candice was staring at me.

For one long, unbearable moment, she said nothing.

Then, with no emotion whatsoever, she finally spoke.

"That was intense."

That was it.

That was all I got.

Not "Wow, I didn't know you felt that way."

Not "I've been thinking about you too."

Not "Maybe we should talk about this."

Just "That was intense."

I stood there, completely stunned.

I had just poured my entire heart out, and that was her response?

I had nothing left to say.

I shoved the letter back in her hands and muttered, "Just think about it."

Then, before I could humiliate myself even further, I got into my car.

The Drive of Shame

I drove home in silence.

No music. No radio.

Just the crushing weight of how badly I had just embarrassed myself.

With every mile, my inner monologue got worse.

Why did you read it out loud?

Why was it six pages?

WHY did you fold it into a heart?!

"That was intense"?! That's all *you got?!*

I had nothing left to give.

Candice had my words.

She had my feelings.

She had everything.

And now?

It was completely up to her.

I told myself it was over.

That I had done everything I could.

But Candice?

Candice wasn't finished with me yet.

The Utah Plan—Was It Really About Land?

I had spent the past few days reliving every second of Memorial Day weekend in my head, trying to figure out what I was supposed to do next.

I later found out Candice and her boyfriend had broken up, but my way to her was in no way clear.

Candice had barely acknowledged me. She had listened to my letter but gave me nothing in return. And then she was just gone.

Back to Idaho.

Back to her life.

And I was left to wonder: Had I just made a complete fool of myself?

I didn't hear from her.

Days passed. Then a week.

And then, finally, one of those short, distant phone calls.

She called me back after a few days, her voice still carrying that same guarded tone I had grown used to. I was just grateful she had called at all.

I asked her about her trip back.

And that's when it happened.

She casually mentioned Clayton.

Clayton.

At first, I thought I had misheard.

But no. She said it again.

Clayton.

And then, just like that, it all made sense.

She had another guy.

It wasn't just that she was unsure about me. She already had a hopeful relationship with someone else.

And the absolute kicker?

The guy's name was Clayton.

I kid you not.

What are the odds?

It was like some cruel cosmic joke.

But here's the thing—Clayton might have had my name, but he did not have my face.

Or my dance moves.

Or my charm.

No, this guy?

This guy was ugly.

Now, look—I'm not one to rip on another man's appearance . . . unless he's standing between me and the love of my life.

And let me tell you, this guy looked like he had just trotted out of a stable.

Horseface Clayton.

That's what I called him in my head. Honestly, he was actually probably pretty good-looking; Candice didn't date ugly guys. But to me he would have to stay Horseface for now.

And somehow, this dude was the one Candice had been waiting for.

While I had been at her house, pouring my heart out under the desert sky, she had been mentally checked out, waiting for him to come pick her up.

He was the plan.

I was some ex-boyfriend who had shown up out of nowhere, throwing six-page love letters around like a lunatic.

And she wasn't waiting for me.

She was waiting for Horseface Clayton.

That thought burned a hole in my chest.

But Then There Was Katie

Katie had been there since the beginning.

She was the one who had brought Candice to the dance where we first met. She was my age, had recently gotten married to a friend of mine, and now lived just down the street from me.

We talked all the time.

And every time Candice and I had one of our short, disappointing phone calls, I would end up talking to Katie later that week.

And without fail, she would tell me the same thing.

"Oh, yeah, I just talked to Candice. She's still so in love with you."

"She tells me all the time how much she loves you."

"She just needs time."

"She's figuring things out."

Now, I was pretty good at reading people. And nothing about Candice's behavior had convinced me that she still had feelings for me.

But why would Katie lie?

Katie was close with Candice. She had no reason to make this up.

And honestly?

I wanted to believe it.

So I did.

Despite all the warning signs.

Despite Clayton—excuse me, Horseface Clayton.

Despite Candice's coldness, despite her avoidance, despite everything telling me I was wasting my time . . .

I let hope win.

So I did the next logical thing.

I made a plan to go to Utah.

Now, on paper, the plan looked perfectly reasonable. I had purchased some land at an auction and had never actually seen it. Utah was right next to Idaho. It only made sense to make a trip out of it.

But let's be honest—this wasn't a real estate trip.

The land didn't matter. Not really.

This was about Candice.

I didn't have a strategy. I didn't have a speech. I had no idea what I was going to say or how I was going to get past the emotional firewall she had built since the breakup.

All I had was a hunch . . . and a heart that wouldn't quit.

I told myself this was fate. That timing was finally working in my favor. That maybe—just maybe—she was waiting for me to show up and prove I still meant it.

But before I even packed a bag, something happened that should've told me exactly where I stood.

After weeks of the usual chasing-Candice routine, I finally got her on the phone. As expected, she was brief, polite, and distant—just enough engagement to say she wasn't completely ignoring me, but not enough to give me any hope.

Still, I had a plan.

I had casually mentioned to her before that I bought some land in Utah at an auction and needed to check it out. Whether I actually needed to see the land was debatable, but at this point, I was using every excuse I could to get myself within a hundred-mile radius of Candice.

So I figured this was my opening.

"Hey, I'll be up in Utah in a couple of weeks. Thought maybe I could swing by and see you while I'm there."

There was a pause.

A long one.

Then Candice, careful and slow, said, "Oh . . . yeah . . . um . . . Unfortunately, I won't actually be in Rexburg that weekend."

I frowned. Of course.

"Oh, really?" I tried to sound casual. "Where are you gonna be?"

"I'll be at my sister's house," she said, as if that were the end of the conversation.

I almost let it go.

Almost.

But then, a light bulb went off.

Twin Falls.

Twin Falls was actually closer to my Utah trip than Rexburg was.

And in that moment, I knew I had her.

"Oh, shoot! Twin Falls is actually even closer to where I'll be! That works out great."

Silence.

The hesitation in her voice was instant. She realized her mistake.

"Oh . . . um . . . yeah . . . Well, I don't think that would work."

I smirked.

She was scrambling now.

"Why not?" I asked, keeping my voice deliberately easygoing.

". . . Because I'll be with my sister."

Now I actually laughed.

"Candice, I met your sister. I was just at your parents' house a few weeks ago for Memorial Day, remember? We all had dinner together. She was great."

More hesitation.

"Yeah . . . I just don't think she'd want that."

She wasn't even trying at this point.

And honestly?

I almost admired the effort.

But at this point, it wasn't just about Candice anymore.

Her parents had fully switched to Team Clay.

And when I mentioned my Utah trip to them at one of our weekly dance lessons, which I started giving them for free, they immediately jumped on board.

"You should absolutely go see her!" her mom said, way too excitedly.

Her dad agreed.

So, with their support, I went straight to the next-best option—Candice's sister.

I called her up and gave my best friendly, harmless guy pitch.

"Hey, I'm gonna be in Utah, and I thought—since I'll be so close—I'd come by for a few days. Would that be okay?"

To my utter shock, she said, "Oh, yeah! No problem. Come on up!"

I was in.

Candice didn't know it yet, but I was coming to Idaho.

And this time, she wasn't getting out of it.

And to soften the blow . . . I had one more move left.

The Flowers That Were Supposed to Fix Everything

If I was going to make this trip work, I needed an opening move. Something that said, *Hey, I know I just kind of invited myself to your sister's house, but I'm still that charming guy you once loved.*

Flowers.

Not just any flowers—the biggest, most ridiculous bouquet money could buy.

I called up the only florist in Rexburg, Idaho, and told them, "Give me the biggest arrangement you've got. The most expensive one. Just make it over the top."

Then, I had them delivered to The Hard Hat, the little restaurant where Candice was working as a server. Right in the middle of her shift.

Subtle? Absolutely not.

The note? Short and to the point:

Looking forward to seeing you. —Clay

Not Clayton. Not my full name. Just Clay.

Because, let's be honest—I wasn't about to risk her thinking these came from Horseface Clayton.

It was a move straight out of the movies. Grand, romantic, undeniable.

It might not have been my worst idea ever . . .

But it definitely didn't put a crack in the Great Wall of China around her heart.

I pulled into her sister's house just after sunset.

It was completely dark.

No porch light. No car in the driveway.

No signs of life.

I checked my directions twice. This was definitely the right house.

I knocked on the door.

No answer.

So I went back to my car and waited.

Five minutes.

Ten.

Twenty.

By the thirty-minute mark, I was starting to wonder if I'd imagined the whole invitation.

Still nothing.

Finally, I pulled out my phone and called Candice.

She picked up.

A small victory.

"Hey," I said, trying to sound casual, despite the fact that I was sitting in an empty driveway like a stray dog. "I just got here."

A long pause.

Then, flatly, she replied,

"Oh. I'm almost there."

A half hour later, she finally arrived. She parked on the street. Not in the driveway, where there was plenty of room.

She got out of her car, looked straight ahead . . . and walked right past me.

The moment Candice walked past me without so much as a glance, I knew I was in trouble.

Not just regular trouble—the kind of trouble where you start questioning every life choice that led you to this exact moment.

She didn't smile. She didn't say hello. She didn't even acknowledge the absurdly large bouquet of flowers I had sent to her workplace earlier that day.

I had driven all this way. I had put everything on the line. I had sent flowers, for crying out loud. And she wasn't even going to say hi?

I stood in the driveway for a moment, taking it all in. Then, trying to recover, I grabbed my bags from the car, walked over to hers, and did what any decent person would do.

I carried her bags inside for her.

She didn't ask me to. She didn't even acknowledge that I was doing it. She just walked into the house like I wasn't right behind her, hauling her things inside like some kind of unpaid bellhop.

I set her bags down in the living room and waited.

Nothing.

Not a thank-you, not a nod, not even an awkward half-smile.

Nothing.

The House of Ice, Part Two

Inside, her sister and brother-in-law were warm and welcoming.

Candice, on the other hand?

Stone cold.

It felt like part two of a night I'd already lived once and that didn't turn out well.

I tried to play it cool—made small talk, helped in the kitchen, pretended I wasn't being systematically avoided. But she was making it obvious: She didn't want me there.

Every time I got close, she moved.

If I sat near her, she got up.

If I walked into the kitchen, she walked out.

Eventually, I gave up and sat on the couch.

She positioned herself at the opposite end—full extension—and picked up a call from some guy.

Loud enough for me to hear. Strategic enough to sting.

She wanted me to feel stupid.

And it worked.

This whole "let's see how miserable I can make Clay feel" act went on for hours.

By the time the evening wound down, I was mentally exhausted.

I had spent the entire night playing an unwinnable game—trying to prove I could handle her ice-cold demeanor without breaking while also desperately hoping for some kind of miracle turnaround.

Spoiler alert: The miracle never came.

As bedtime approached, her sister showed me to the guest room. Candice had already disappeared into her own room without a single word to me.

I stood in the hallway for a moment, staring down at the floor, trying to process everything.

This trip had been a mistake.

A huge mistake.

I felt defeated. Completely and utterly defeated.

For the first time since deciding I would either marry Candice or watch her marry someone else, I wondered if I had completely misread everything.

Maybe this was it.

Maybe I should just accept it and move on.

I turned off the light, laid down in bed, and stared at the ceiling.

And then, out of sheer desperation, I did the only thing I could think of.

I prayed. "Heavenly Father, what am I doing here? What have I done?"

And that's when the answer came.

It wasn't what I expected.

It wasn't comforting.

It wasn't reassuring.

It was insane.

"Go pray with her."

I froze.

No. Absolutely not.

That couldn't be right.

There was no way—*no way*—God was actually telling me to go pray with Candice right now.

I squeezed my eyes shut, shaking my head.

"There is no possible way you want me to get up, walk down the hallway, knock on her door, and ask her to pray with me—after everything that just happened. You cannot be serious."

But the feeling wouldn't go away.

The more I resisted, the stronger it got.

And so, against every ounce of logic and self-preservation I had left, I got out of bed, walked down the hall, and . . .

There are moments in life when you realize, with absolute certainty, that you are about to do something colossally stupid.

This was one of those moments.

I stood outside Candice's door, my hand hovering over the wood, my brain screaming at me to turn around.

No. Nope. This is a bad idea. Turn around; walk away. You've embarrassed yourself enough for one day. Heck, for one lifetime. Just cut your losses and go to bed.

I ignored myself.

And instead, I knocked.

From inside, her voice came—flat, unimpressed, and the kind of tone that made me question every decision I had ever made leading up to this moment.

"What do you want?" Somehow she knew it was me at the door.

Oh boy.

That's when the panic set in.

I could still turn back. Pretend I was knocking on the wrong door. Act like I had a question about towels or needed to borrow toothpaste. Anything—*anything*—other than what I was about to say.

But no. I was already here.

So, like the absolute fool that I was, I blurted out,

"Uh . . . Would you . . . Would you pray with me?"

Silence.

The kind of silence that fills your lungs with regret and makes you wish you could rewind time and slap yourself before you even formed the thought.

I stared at the door, waiting.

Was she about to laugh at me? Tell me to get lost? Open the door just to slam it in my face?

Then, finally, she spoke.

"Sure, come in."

I almost fell over.

Not because she said yes, but because of how she said it.

No warmth. No emotion. No softness. Just . . . confusion. Like she was genuinely baffled by what I was doing but, at the same time, weirdly intrigued.

As I walked in, she added,

"Do you want me to say it?"

Her tone made it clear—she wanted this to be over as quickly as possible.

I scrambled to shake my head.

"No, no. I'll say it."

She didn't even move.

Didn't sit up. Didn't adjust her pillow. Just laid there on the bed, watching me like I was some bizarre animal that had wandered into her room by accident.

I hesitated for a second, then walked in and sat at the very edge of the bed—as stiff as a board—folding my arms like I was a little kid saying bedtime prayers.

And then?

I squeezed my eyes shut so tight, I'm pretty sure I could see the next dimension.

I was not about to risk seeing her face.

Because if she was smirking?

If she was rolling her eyes?

If she looked even remotely amused by my pathetic attempt at a last ditch Hail Mary?

I was going to absolutely lose it.

So I kept my eyes shut and got straight to the point.

"Heavenly Father, if you could just allow us to be friends, that would be great."

That was it.

That was the whole prayer.

I didn't ask for guidance.

I didn't ask for her to see how much I cared.

I didn't ask for wisdom or patience or anything remotely meaningful.

Nope.

I just sat there, like an absolute desperate idiot, asking God for a single, bare-minimum friendship.

When I opened my eyes, Candice was silent.

Not a word.

Not a single, thoughtful "Thank you for that."

Not a quiet "I appreciate that."

Not anything except a flat, simple, unenthusiastic "Thanks."

And that was the moment I realized I really was that stupid.

I had just hit a new personal low—a grown man, literally begging God out loud for the privilege of being friend-zoned.

I shot up from the bed so fast, you would've thought it had caught fire.

"Good night," I said quickly.

And before she could say anything else, I turned and practically fled the room.

The hallway back to my room felt like a mile long.

With every step, my brain replayed the moment in excruciating detail.

Why did I do that?

Why do I keep doing this?

What is wrong with me?!

I should have felt humiliated.

I should have been done.

But instead, one stubborn thought kept me moving forward:

At least I showed her that I would pray with her for the rest of her life.

Maybe she thought I was ridiculous.

Maybe she was still just tolerating me.

Maybe she was just waiting for me to finally give up.

But deep down?

I think she was surprised that I just wouldn't let go.

I reached my room, collapsed onto the bed, and stared at the ceiling.

What had I just done?

Had I ruined everything?

Was this the final nail in the coffin of Candice ever wanting anything to do with me?

I had no idea.

But one thing was clear.

If I was going to win this girl back . . .

I was going to have to survive whatever humiliation came next.

The Morning After—Any Sign of a Breakthrough?

I woke up feeling genuinely excited.

Despite everything—the cold shoulder, the awkward prayer moment, the fact that she had basically treated me like a stray dog the night before—I was still hopeful.

Today was the day.

When I told Candice about the trip over the phone, she had agreed to let me take her out.. And I had a full day planned.

Roller-skating. Waterfalls. Lunch. Dinner. Everything.

I walked into the kitchen, feeling pretty good about life, and found Candice sitting at the table, eating breakfast.

I smiled.

"Ready for today?" I asked, already picturing how this day was about to turn everything around.

She looked up at me with zero recognition in her eyes.

"For what?"

I almost choked on air.

For what?

For what?!

I forced a smile, ignoring the panic setting in.

"You know . . . our date?"

Candice frowned slightly, like she was really trying to remember.

Then, finally—finally—she gave a small nod.

"Oh . . . right. I forgot."

Forgot?!

I stared at her. I had spent weeks looking forward to this day. I had planned every detail.

And she had just . . . forgotten?

I was about to try and recover when her sister, who had been watching this slow-motion train wreck unfold, decided to step in.

"So, what are you guys doing today?" she asked, clearly trying to help me out.

I jumped on the opportunity.

"Well," I said, glancing at Candice, "I was thinking we could go roller-skating, maybe check out the waterfalls, grab some lunch—"

Before I could even finish, she shook her head.

"Yeah . . . I don't think I can."

I blinked.

What?

She took another bite of breakfast, completely unfazed by the emotional damage she was inflicting.

"I'm gonna go running with my sister this morning," she said casually.

I was not prepared for this.

Running?

This was not part of the plan.

Her sister, the only person in this house who still seemed to be on my side, tried again.

"Well, why don't you come with us?"

Candice turned and looked right at me, waiting for my answer.

Now, I hated running.

Not mildly disliked. Not avoided when possible.

Hated.

When I wrestled in high school, running was the worst part of practice.

I was fine slamming people into the mat. I was fine pushing myself to exhaustion in a match.

But running?

We ran forever.

And I quickly learned I was not built for it.

I was always in the back of the pack, struggling with the heavyweights, wondering why on earth this was part of wrestling training in the first place.

So when Candice and her sister casually suggested that I run with them, every muscle in my body protested.

But my brain?

My brain said, *You have no choice. You are running today.*

I forced a grin. "Oh, I love running."

Lie.

Candice raised an eyebrow. She had to have known it was a lie.

But she didn't call me on it.

She just shrugged, finished her breakfast, and stood up.

"Alright. Let's go, then."

And just like that, my meticulously planned day was already falling apart.

The Run That Nearly Killed Me

We arrived at the park, and I immediately realized this was a mistake.

The track was paved, looping around a massive open field. Candice's sister wasn't much of a runner, so her plan was to walk. Candice, on the other hand? She was about to put me through absolute hell.

She ran almost every day—seven miles a day, to be exact.

I, on the other hand, only ran when absolutely necessary. Like when being chased. By a bear. Or a swarm of bees. Or a really aggressive mall kiosk worker.

But I wasn't about to admit that.

So, when Candice asked, "Are you running with me?" I lied straight to her face.

"Oh, yeah, I love running."

She grinned, clearly not believing me, but shrugged and took off at an easy, effortless pace.

I kept up.

For about half a mile.

Then I started to feel it.

By a mile, I was questioning every life decision I had ever made.

By a mile and a half, my lungs were betraying me.

By two miles, I was done.

Casually—very casually—I slowed to a jog, then to a walk, and then, as if this had been my plan all along, I fell in step with Candice's sister.

"Change of strategy?" she asked, amused.

"Oh, yeah." I nodded, trying to sound convincing. "I just figured I'd keep you company."

I refused to acknowledge that Candice, at this point, had lapped me three times and showed no signs of stopping.

Her sister smirked. She knew exactly what had happened.

I tried to keep the conversation light, masking the fact that I was about to collapse.

Meanwhile, Candice?

She kept going.

Not just going—flying.

She looked annoyingly graceful, like this was just a warm-up jog.

I watched in horror as she disappeared into the distance, then reappeared as she lapped me.

Then she lapped me again.

And again.

At one point, she jogged backward for a few steps, smiling, and called out, "Doing okay?"

I wanted to lie.

To pretend that I was fine.

Instead, I just gave a thumbs-up because I couldn't breathe enough to talk.

By the time Candice finished her seven miles, I had barely walked another mile.

I could see the amusement in her face as we got back to where the car was parked.

"You love running, huh?" she teased, smirking.

I wheezed, still gasping for breath.

"Oh, yeah. Love it."

She laughed. Not helping my cause.

Then, as if she hadn't already humiliated me enough, she did something that nearly broke me completely.

Rather than getting in the car with me, which might have killed her, she stretched her arms over her head, shook out her legs, and said,

"I think I'll just run back. It's only a few more miles."

I stared at her.

She was serious.

She had already run seven miles, and now she was running more.

I had barely survived walking, and yes, I was completely outmatched in every possible way.

But little did she know . . .

I could take a beating.

And I wasn't going anywhere.

Desperation in the Passenger Seat

I barely managed to drag myself to the car, throw open the door, and collapse into the passenger seat next to Candice's sister. I was done.

Physically? Destroyed.

Emotionally? Teetering on the edge of insanity.

Mentally? Desperate for answers.

As we pulled away from the park, I watched through the side mirror as Candice disappeared into the distance—running, again, like some kind of superhuman.

I let out a long, defeated sigh and, without even thinking, the words just fell out of my mouth.

"Do I have any chance with your sister?"

It wasn't planned.

It wasn't smooth.

It wasn't anything but pure exhaustion and desperation leaking out of me.

It was like that moment from *Dumb and Dumber*—I was practically begging for her to tell me I had a one-in-a-million shot.

Candice's sister—bless her kind soul—did not laugh at me.

She could have; she should have.

Instead, she turned to me with genuine kindness and said, "I honestly have no idea."

I blinked.

That wasn't good, but it wasn't bad either.

She wasn't giving me false hope.

But she wasn't shutting the door completely either.

It was so sweet of her to say it that way.

Still, I couldn't help but feel like a complete fool.

Here I was, a grown man, practically begging Candice's sister for information—grasping at straws, hoping for anything.

But instead of giving up, instead of taking this as a sign to move on, instead of accepting what should have been obvious by now . . .

I doubled down.

Because even if no one knew where this was going . . .

I was still all in.

Back at the House—One More Attempt at a Date

By the time we got back to the house, I had recovered just enough to put my real plan into action.

This was it. Date time.

I had waited all morning through a brutal run, a humbling car ride, and an exhausting battle with my own doubts.

Now?

It was my moment.

I walked into the house, took a deep breath, found Candice, and with all the confidence I could muster, I said,

"All right! So, are you ready for our date?"

She barely looked up.

"Oh . . . yeah. My brother-in-law actually wanted to take you golfing."

Silence.

. . . Excuse me?

I blinked.

That was not the plan.

She didn't say, "I'd rather do something else."

She didn't say, "I'm not feeling up for it."

She didn't even say, "I changed my mind."

She outsourced me.

Like I was a pesky obligation that she had just handed off to someone else.

I didn't even know what to say.

I just stood there, processing.

Her brother-in-law, on the other hand?

Oh, he was pumped.

He clapped me on the back and said, "Yeah, man! Let's go golfing!"

I glanced at Candice.

She gave nothing away.

No guilt.

No sympathy.

Not even an ounce of "Maybe I should feel bad about this."

And that's when it hit me.

I had no choice.

If I made a big deal about it? I'd look pathetic.

If I sulked? I'd look even worse.

If I said no? I'd lose whatever little ground I had left.

So, with as much fake enthusiasm as I could possibly gather, I forced a smile and nodded. "I'm in! Let's tee up some magic."

And with that, my long-awaited date with Candice turned into a full-blown bromance outing.

I didn't know whether to laugh or cry.

But one thing was for sure . . .

I was not giving up yet.

The Golf Game—A Surprisingly Good Time

If Candice thought sending me off to golf with her brother-in-law would deter me, she clearly didn't understand just how stubborn I was.

Fine. You don't want to go on a date with me? I'll win over your family instead.

And let me tell you, her brother-in-law and I had an absolute blast.

From the moment we hit the course, it was nonstop laughs. The guy was awesome—easygoing, hilarious, and just as competitive as I was.

We decided to play best ball (which, thankfully, meant I had a chance to not embarrass myself completely).

Now, to be clear—

I wasn't terrible at golf.

I wasn't great, either.

Let's just say I was slightly better at golf than I was at running.

Which, after that morning's humiliating jog, wasn't saying much.

But with best ball, we actually made a solid team.

We cracked jokes.

We made fun of each other's swings.

By the time we got to the back nine, we were best friends.

And the whole time, in the back of my mind, I kept thinking,

All right, Candice. You can try to push me away all you want, but I'm about to become a permanent part of your family.

After eighteen holes, a whole lot of laughing, and a newfound brotherhood, we finally headed back to the house.

And you better believe—I was going to ask Candice out again.

Back from Golf—The Final Attempt at a Date

As much fun as I was having with Candice's brother-in-law, there was one thing weighing on my mind the entire time—

This was eating up precious time I could have been spending with Candice.

Sure, I had won over her brother-in-law. That was great. Another point in my favor, but I wasn't there to impress him.

I was there for her.

And as much as I enjoyed the bromance, every second on that golf course felt like time slipping away.

So the moment we wrapped up the final hole, I wasted no time.

We drove back to the house, and before I even stepped inside, I was already plotting my next move.

Now, I wasn't stupid. I knew she wasn't exactly thrilled about a date with me. But I also knew something else—Candice loved Johnny Carino's.

And lucky for me, Twin Falls had one.

I had a secret weapon: pasta.

Because no matter how much she wanted to keep me at arm's length, I knew she couldn't resist Johnny Carino's.

I walked in, saw her across the room, and with renewed determination, I asked,

"Hey, so . . . Can I take you out now, maybe Johnny Carino's?"

I braced myself.

Waited for another excuse.

And to my utter shock—

She hesitated.

Then, with reluctance, she sighed. "Fine, just dinner."

I had made progress. Sort of.

Candice hadn't agreed to a date, but she had agreed to let me take her to dinner.

That was good enough for me.

That tiny victory, however, quickly turned into another test of patience.

Killing Time with the Cutest Kid in Idaho

Candice needed to get ready.

Now, I grew up with sisters. I knew that "getting ready" wasn't always a quick process.

But I wasn't prepared for this.

Five minutes passed.

Then ten.

Fifteen.

I started pacing.

Her sister and brother-in-law sat on the couch, watching me struggle with visible amusement.

"She's taking her time, huh?" her sister teased.

I forced a casual shrug. "Oh, no big deal. I'm sure she'll be ready soon."

That was a bald-faced lie.

Because twenty minutes passed. Then thirty.

I needed a distraction.

That's when I saw her nephew.

Now, I absolutely love kids. Always have. And this little boy? One of the cutest kids I had ever seen.

Thick, curly blond hair. Giant blue eyes.

And most importantly? He was just as eager to play as I was.

So I took him outside, and we started playing catch in the front yard.

For a kid so little, he had a solid throw, and an even better laugh. We were having a blast.

At some point, I completely forgot why I was even waiting.

But then, out of the corner of my eye, I saw Candice finally step outside.

And just like that, my frustration vanished.

Even after everything—the avoidance, the cold shoulder, the relentless emotional obstacle course—I still thought she was worth every second of waiting.

The Drive to Dinner—A Strategic Detour

When Candice finally emerged, ready for dinner, she looked stunning. Not that I was shocked—Candice always looked incredible—but there was something about her that night that made it feel like we were actually on a date, even though she had done everything in her power to make sure it didn't feel that way.

I, of course, had strategically chosen Johnny Carino's because I knew it was her favorite restaurant in Twin Falls. I needed every advantage I could get, and food was definitely one of them.

But there was one more move I had to make before dinner.

As we got in the car and pulled out of the driveway, I decided to lay it on thick.

"Hey, before we go eat, we should stop by Shoshone Falls real quick." I said it so casually, like it was an afterthought, but I knew exactly what I was doing.

Candice immediately gave me a look.

A look that said, *Oh no, what are you up to?*

I pressed on before she could shut it down.

"I mean, it would be a real shame to come all this way and not stop and see them. They're called the Niagara of the West, you know. I've never been. Seems like a waste to skip it."

I could see her wheels turning.

She knew.

She knew I had spent all day trying to get time with her. She knew this wasn't just about a waterfall. She knew this was a move.

But I had chosen something she couldn't say no to.

Her hesitation told me I was right.

She wanted to say no. But she couldn't.

"... Fine."

That was it. No excitement. No curiosity. Just, fine.

I wasn't deterred.

This was going to work.

Or at least, that's what I told myself.

When we arrived at the falls, the sun was just starting to set, casting that perfect golden glow over everything. It was absolutely beautiful. A scene straight out of a movie.

The perfect place for a romantic moment.

Unfortunately, Candice did not get that memo.

I parked the car, and we got out, standing side by side at the overlook, watching the waterfall crash down below.

Hoping that she could see how great this was.

Candice wasn't ready to admit it.

That much was obvious.

But what really threw me off wasn't just her hesitation—it was how mean she was being.

Candice is not a mean person. In fact, she might be the kindest person I've ever met. Yet, for some reason, here, with me, she was sharp. Dismissive. Cold.

And I couldn't put my finger on why.

It wasn't just that she was trying to keep me at a distance—she was going out of her way to make me feel like an idiot for even trying.

I had to assume it was self-preservation. I had broken her heart before. And maybe, just maybe, she was determined not to let me do it again.

Still, I wasn't about to back down just because she was being difficult.

I had come too far.

Standing there at Shoshone Falls, I had one goal in mind—get her to open up, even just a little.

So, I asked, "What do you want in a husband?"

I expected her to hesitate. Maybe deflect.

Instead, she answered immediately.

Like she had rehearsed it.

"Well, I want someone tall. He has to have blue eyes. He needs to love to dance. He has to be an entrepreneur, good with people, and really love life."

She listed it off like she was reading a grocery list.

And the second she finished, something clicked in my brain.

She had just described me.

Every. Single. Thing.

I almost laughed.

There was no way she had done that on purpose.

So I just stood there, watching her, waiting for her to realize it.

But she just stared at the waterfall, completely unaffected, like she hadn't just obliterated her own defense mechanism.

I could have let it slide.

I could have let the moment pass.

But I didn't.

Instead, I smirked and said, "Well . . . I've got all of those things."

And that?

That was too much for her.

She immediately turned on her heel and started walking back toward the car.

"Okay, dinnertime."

That was all she said.

No response.

No argument.

Just a full-blown retreat.

I watched her for a second, trying to decide if I should call her out on it.

But I didn't.

Because deep down, I knew—Candice was in trouble.

She wasn't just fighting me.

She was fighting herself.

And I had a feeling she wasn't going to win.

Chapter 15

The Car Ride and Dinner: The Brutal Honesty Moment

The moment Candice and I got into the car, I knew I had her cornered—literally. There was nowhere for her to run, no sudden tasks to complete, no convenient excuses to slip away. She was stuck with me for the duration of this ride, and for the first time all day, I had her full attention.

Or so I thought.

She sat in the passenger seat, looking out the window, responding to my conversation with short, clipped answers. She wasn't avoiding me—there was nowhere to go—but she was doing everything she could to keep her walls up. It wasn't full-on hostility, but it was definitely a far cry from the Candice I once knew.

I kept the conversation light, hoping to ease her into something more natural. We talked about Idaho, her classes, random things we used to joke about, but something was different. She wasn't laughing at my jokes like before. She wasn't teasing me back. She was polite but detached.

Finally, I couldn't take it anymore.

We were halfway to dinner when I asked, "Why are you so mean to me?"

She turned to me, startled, and for the first time in the entire car ride, I saw the Candice I remembered. The Candice who hated being unkind. The Candice who didn't enjoy hurting people.

She hesitated.

Then she sighed and said, "I don't want you to think I like you."

Ouch.

It hit me like a brick to the face. She was holding on to everything that had happened before—the breakup, the time apart, the uncertainty. She didn't trust me. She didn't want to open herself up to me again, not if there was a chance I could hurt her like before.

And I got it.

But I also knew one thing for certain: I wasn't walking away this time.

I smiled, trying to keep my voice light even though I felt like I had just been gutted. "Okay, well, I promise, no matter how you act, I won't assume you like me. But I can't promise that I'll ever stop liking you. Are you okay with that?"

She paused. I could see the wheels turning in her mind, as if she were trying to find a reason to argue. But then, almost reluctantly, she nodded.

"Yeah, I can do that."

And just like that, everything changed.

By the time we got to the restaurant, the energy between us had shifted. She wasn't pushing me away anymore. She let herself relax just a little, and for the first time in a long time, I felt like we were on even ground.

We sat down at Johnny Carino's—and for the first time since dessert with a fender bender, we had a real conversation. We talked, we laughed, and for a moment, it felt like old times.

I didn't know what would happen after tonight, but I knew one thing for sure: This was a step in the right direction.

After dinner, we drove back to her sister's house.

Unlike the ride to the restaurant, this drive wasn't filled with awkwardness or tension. It was . . . calm. We weren't talking much, but it wasn't uncomfortable. There was something about the silence that felt peaceful—like a truce had been called.

I didn't push conversation. I didn't try to force a moment.

When we got back to her sister's house, I expected her to disappear to her room like she had been doing all weekend.

But she didn't.

Instead, she stayed in the living room with her sister, her brother-in-law, and me.

We hung out. Talked. Put on a movie.

For the first time in a long time, it felt easy.

I wasn't some desperate guy chasing after a girl who wanted nothing to do with him. I wasn't fighting against a wall she had built between us.

We were just two people sitting on a couch, watching a movie.

It was like old times.

Maybe not in the way I had imagined or hoped, but still, it was something.

Eventually, the night wound down, and we all went to bed.

I lay there in the dark, staring up at the ceiling, thinking about everything that had happened over the last twenty-four hours.

Candice had been distant, cold, and uninterested for months.

And now?

She had agreed to dinner. She had laughed at my jokes. She had actually enjoyed my company.

And maybe, just maybe, that meant there was still a chance.

That night, my prayers weren't desperate like they had been before.

They were filled with gratitude.

I had prayed to just be friends with Candice again.

And tonight, the Lord had given me exactly that.

The Goodbye and the CD

The morning was quiet. Too quiet, honestly. After everything—the cold shoulders, the awkward dinner, the emotional whiplash—I wasn't sure what to expect. A meltdown? A breakthrough? A hug followed by a restraining order?

Instead, it was weirdly peaceful.

We weren't exactly riding off into the sunset, but we also weren't pretending the weekend hadn't happened. It wasn't the perfect ending to a love story, but it also wasn't a flaming wreck on the side of the highway. And for us? That was progress.

We were both leaving that morning—Candice heading back to Rexburg, me making the long, reflective drive to Tucson. We stood in the driveway for a minute, that crisp Idaho air hanging between us like one last, awkward pause.

I didn't know what the weekend had changed, if anything. Would we keep talking? Would she ghost me again? Had I made progress—or just wasted a tank of gas and three days of emotional vulnerability?

I had one last card to play.

A few days earlier, I had what felt like a bold, romantic idea: make her a mix CD.

Yes, Gen Z, a CD. Short for *compact disc.* It's like a Spotify playlist with commitment issues and no shuffle button. Back in the day, if you wanted to express your feelings through music, you didn't send a link—you *burned* a disc, wrote on it with a Sharpie, and hoped it didn't skip on Track 7.

Naturally, I ran the idea by Katie first.

She didn't even hesitate. "That's adorable. Girls love stuff like that."

And maybe they did. But after everything—after the letter, the trip, and a late-night prayer session that felt like an emotional Hail Mary—I wasn't sure if one more grand gesture was sweet . . . or just excessive.

So I left it in the car. Just in case I chickened out.

And standing there, looking at Candice, I nearly did. But then I blurted it out: "Hey . . . So I made you a CD. Do you want it?"

Her eyes lit up.

Not in a polite, "Thanks, that's cute" kind of way. I mean *lit up.*

"You made me a CD?" she said, her whole face softening.

I nodded, suddenly nervous again. "Yeah . . . just some songs that remind me of you."

She beamed. "Yes. I want it."

She took it, looked down at the case, and then—no joke—hugged it to her chest like it was something special.

After months of coldness, mixed signals, and total emotional confusion, that smile made it all worth it.

She didn't pretend it didn't matter. She didn't act cool or play it down. She just *liked it.* And for the first time in a long time, I felt like I had finally done something right.

She looked back up and said, "I'll listen to it."

That's all she said.

And honestly? That was enough.

I got into my car first and pulled away. I'm not sure when she left. For all I know, she stood there a while longer, CD still clutched to her chest, figuring out what it all meant.

Or maybe she didn't.

I didn't know where we stood.

But for the first time in a long time . . .

I didn't feel crazy.

I felt hopeful.

The Unexpected Call

I had been on the road for about thirty minutes, watching the Idaho landscape roll by, my mind replaying every moment from the weekend.

I had gotten exactly what I prayed for—Candice and I were friends again.

Still, as I drove, I couldn't shake the feeling that this might be the last time I'd see her like this. Sure, we had fun at dinner, but Candice had a life in Idaho. Would she just go back to pretending I didn't exist once I left?

Then my phone rang.

I glanced at the screen.

Candice.

I nearly swerved off the road.

Candice never called me first. Ever. At least not since I broke her heart the first time.

In fact, the only times I had seen her name pop up on my screen were when she was returning a call days after I had left a message.

My first thought?

I forgot something.

Her sister probably noticed something embarrassing I left behind— maybe a sock, maybe my toothbrush—maybe my underwear.

That had to be it.

I let the phone ring a couple of times, just to play it cool. Then, finally, I answered.

"Hello?"

She hesitated.

Then, in a tone I hadn't heard in years—one that was soft, almost playful—she asked, "What if I really start liking you?"

The words hit me like a bolt of lightning.

This. This was it. This was the moment.

I had spent months chasing her, convincing myself that if I just stayed patient, if I just stuck around long enough, she'd remember.

And now, here she was.

Saying it out loud.

Trying to sound casual.

But I knew what this meant.

I had her.

I had her right there.

I forced myself to play it cool.

"Well," I said, smiling so hard my face hurt, "I guess we'll just have to see how that goes."

She laughed, and for the first time in a long time, Candice sounded happy to be talking to me.

I hung up the phone and gripped the steering wheel with both hands, trying to process what had just happened.

I had spent months convincing myself that I could read between the lines—that deep down, Candice still had feelings for me.

But every sign had told me the opposite.

The cold shoulders. The ignored calls. The way she avoided me at every turn.

I had no real proof.

Until now.

I replayed the conversation in my head, hanging on to every word.

"What if I really start liking you?"

She hadn't said, "What if I start thinking about you again?"

She hadn't said, "What if I regret how I treated you?"

She had said, "What if I really start liking you?"

That wasn't a maybe statement. That wasn't a hypothetical.

That was a confession.

And in that moment, I knew.

This wasn't just a trip where I had successfully reentered her life.

This wasn't just about getting back into the friend zone and hoping for the best.

Candice felt something again.

I could tell by her voice—by the way she asked the question like she was testing the waters.

She was scared.

She didn't trust it yet.

And honestly? I didn't blame her.

I had broken her heart once before.

But I also knew something else . . .

I wasn't the same guy who'd let her go the first time.

I wasn't going to make that mistake again.

This time, I would be patient. I would give her space. I would let her come to me.

Because for the first time since we reconnected, I wasn't just chasing a dream.

I wasn't just hoping I had a chance.

I knew—deep in my bones—that she was coming back to me.

And this time?

I wouldn't let her go.

For the next month, I kept things casual. I wasn't about to ruin this by coming on too strong. I called her every few days—never too much, never too little. Just enough to remind her that I was there, that I wasn't going anywhere, and that I still cared.

The biggest difference?

She actually picked up.

She still had her walls up, but she wasn't avoiding me anymore. She was busy, and I was busy, but we made time to stay connected. The conversations weren't long or deep, but they were consistent. And in those moments, I could feel something shifting.

I wasn't just the guy she used to date anymore.

I was becoming part of her life again.

I had no idea where this was going, but I knew one thing—I had patience.

And I was willing to wait.

Chapter 16

The Road to Utah: When Her Parents Teamed Up with Me

A month had passed since the unexpected call, and while Candice and I had been talking regularly, we were still stuck in this weird in-between phase—closer than before but nowhere near where I wanted to be.

Then, out of nowhere, her parents handed me the perfect opportunity.

Candice was coming home.

Well, not quite home—her parents were planning a trip to Utah to see family, and from there, they were going to drive her back to Tucson for the summer.

And her parents?

They wanted me to come along.

"You should drive up there with us," her mom suggested casually during one of our dance lessons. "It'd be so much safer for Candice to have someone drive back with her."

I had to keep myself from grinning.

This was perfect.

An entire road trip with Candice? Hours stuck in a car together? Her parents rooting for me? It was almost too good to be true.

Of course, Candice had no idea about this plan yet.

Her mom had said it like it was already set in stone, but I knew better. If Candice thought for a second that this was some elaborate scheme to get us back together, she'd shut it down before it even started.

So I played it cool.

"Sounds like a great idea," I said. "But only if Candice is okay with it."

Her mom waved a hand, like that was a minor detail. "Oh, she'll be fine with it."

I wasn't so sure.

And I was right to be skeptical.

The moment Candice found out, she called me.

"You're driving to Utah?" she asked, her voice neutral.

"Yeah," I said, keeping my tone just as casual. "Your parents thought it'd be a good idea."

Silence.

Then, finally:

"Oh . . . Okay."

That was it.

No protest. No rejection. No enthusiasm, either.

But she wasn't saying no.

Which meant I was in.

And once again, I was on my way to see Candice—whether she was ready for it or not.

Déjà Vu—Cold Shoulders in Utah

The drive up to Utah with her parents was great. I had already built a solid relationship with them, so we talked, laughed, and enjoyed the trip. The entire ride up, I thought this was going to be different. Candice and I have been talking. She called me first after I left Idaho. Things were finally shifting.

But the moment we arrived at her Aunt Jan's house?

It was like I had stepped into a time loop.

Candice greeted her parents warmly, hugged her aunt, smiled at her cousins. And me?

Nothing.

No hug. No real acknowledgment. Barely a hello.

Here we go again.

I had just spent the last month thinking we were making progress, only to find myself right back where I started.

Her dad must have noticed, because later that evening, he walked by me, smirking, and muttered a line straight out of *A Knight's Tale*: "There's the love of your life . . . and oh, how you hate her."

I cracked up because, honestly, he wasn't wrong.

Candice, meanwhile, continued her flawless avoidance strategy.

If I walked into a room, she left.

If I sat near her, she found something urgent to do elsewhere.

If we made eye contact, she looked away faster than I thought was humanly possible.

It was the Memorial Day barbecue all over again, except now, I was in a different state with a nine-hour car ride looming ahead.

I had two options.

I could wallow in self-pity, wondering why she was back to acting like I barely existed.

Or I could do what I always did—win over the people around her until she had no choice but to acknowledge me.

So I turned up the charm.

Her Aunt Jan? Loved me.

Her cousins? They thought I was great.

Her parents? Well, they were already on Team Clay.

Candice?

Still ice cold.

At one point, her dad passed by me again, shook his head, and said, "Still nothing?"

I just laughed and shrugged.

But deep down, I was frustrated.

Was this how it was always going to be? Months of warmth, followed by a sudden freeze-out?

I knew I couldn't push her. I knew she had her reasons.

But man, was I getting tired of this game.

Then, I had an idea.

If there was one thing I knew about Candice, it was that she loved to dance.

And lucky for her?

So did I.

The Dance Lesson—My Secret Weapon

I caught Candice early the next morning, just before she could disappear into another busy day of avoiding me.

She had no excuses this time.

The air was cool, the morning sun barely peeking over the horizon, casting long shadows over the lawn. It was the perfect moment, the perfect opportunity.

I took it.

"How about a dance lesson?" I asked, throwing it out casually, like I hadn't been planning it since the moment I woke up.

She blinked, caught off guard.

"Right now?" she asked, skeptical.

"Yeah," I shrugged, playing it cool. "You've been learning two-step, right? Let me see what you've got."

I could see her debating. The Candice that had spent the last few days keeping me at arm's length wanted to say no. But the Candice that loved dancing, that knew how good I was, that had spent months getting better at something I had already mastered?

She wanted to prove herself.

". . . Okay," she said finally.

And just like that, we were standing in the grass, the world still quiet around us. I stepped toward her and held out my hand. She hesitated for the briefest moment before placing hers in mine.

The second I pulled her in, everything else faded away. We moved together like we had never stopped.

It was easy. Effortless.

She followed every step like she had been made for it, and I led like I had been waiting for this moment my entire life. I spun her, dipped her, pushed the boundaries just enough to remind her that this—this was what we had always done best.

She was laughing now, shaking her head, the morning light catching in her hair as we twirled.

We danced for nearly an hour, and in that time, I wasn't just some guy chasing her anymore. I was her Clay. The guy she hadn't stopped thinking about.

When we finally stopped, I suggested a walk—partly to cool down, but mostly because I knew how much she loved it. Walking was her thing. Her reset. Her quiet place.

And somewhere in those first few steps—she reached out and grabbed my hand.

I nearly stopped mid-stride. She had done it instinctively, naturally—like she *wanted* to. And I didn't let go.

But just as fast as the moment had come, it vanished.

Candice suddenly pulled back, dropping my hand like it was on fire.

"I think we're moving too fast," she said quickly, stepping away.

There it was. Classic Candice.

I exhaled and nodded. "Okay," I said, like it didn't kill me just a little bit inside. "Whatever you're comfortable with."

She gave me a small smile—soft, almost grateful.

And yeah, it stung.

But I could tell . . . something had shifted.

That short walk—just a casual two or three miles for Candice—felt like a marathon for me. But I wasn't upset. I wasn't discouraged.

Because even though I'm pretty sure we broke up four or five times during that walk . . . we also laughed. We talked. We teased each other like old times.

And even though she pulled away—again—I knew what had just happened.

She was losing the battle.

The one she'd been fighting so hard.

Trying to convince herself she didn't love me.

But for a few minutes, she forgot to fight it.

And I could feel it.

I was getting closer.

When we got back to the house, she disappeared into another room, and I found myself in the hallway just as her dad walked by.

He gave me a sideways glance and asked, "Did you kiss her yet?"

I shook my head. "Nope. I think there might be something wrong with your daughter."

Without missing a beat, he fired back with that classic dry wit:

"There goes the love of your life . . . and oh, how you hate her."

The Van Ride That Changed Everything

I climbed into the back row of the old Astro van, sitting alone for a moment while everyone else gathered their things. It had been a long day—a roller coaster of emotions, small victories, and even more setbacks.

As I sat there, Candice's mom suddenly poked her head inside. She was a striking woman—fit, petite like Candice, with dark-red hair and freckles. But what I loved most about her was that, like me, she always just said what was on her mind.

She took one look at me, tilted her head, and smirked.

"Well? How's it going?"

I let out a breath, gave her a half smile, and replied with complete honesty: "I have no idea. I actually think your daughter might be crazy."

She burst into laughter.

And then, without missing a beat, she said, "Oh, that's just because she's PMSing. Don't worry about it."

I stared at her for a second, processing what she had just said and surprised that she would say that.

And suddenly—everything made sense.

It was like the final missing puzzle piece snapped into place.

Now, I wasn't new to this concept. I had a mother. I had sisters. I had spent enough time around women to understand that sometimes, the world had simply treated them unfairly with hormones. And Candice, as much as she tried to control it, was not immune.

With that, the last bit of anxiety I had about the day melted away.

I wasn't in trouble. I wasn't losing her again.

I just had to ride this out.

As everyone piled into the Astro van, I sat in the very back, still processing Candice's mom's casual yet oddly reassuring comment. It felt like a weight had been lifted, but I wasn't entirely sure where things stood with Candice.

Her mom took the front passenger seat, Candice's uncle and aunt slid into the middle rows, Candice climbed in beside me, and her cousins filled the rest of the seats so we were packed full. I could feel the warmth of her presence next to me, but she was playing it cool. No hand-holding. No looking my way. Just sitting there, quiet, like we hadn't just been through one of the most emotionally confusing weekends of my life.

Then, just as we were about to pull out of the driveway, her mom suddenly turned in her seat, looked straight at the two of us, and said,

"So what's going on with you two?"

Silence.

I wasn't sure how to answer. Was this a trick question? A trap? A test? I opened my mouth, but before I could even attempt to put together some kind of explanation—

Candice, in the most nonchalant, matter-of-fact tone I had ever heard, said, "Oh, we're boyfriend and girlfriend."

I nearly choked.

Excuse me?

Boyfriend and girlfriend? Since when?!

Just this morning, we had broken up five different times during our walk!

I turned to look at her, but she was acting like this was old news. Like we had always been boyfriend and girlfriend, and the past months of my emotional torment had all been a fever dream.

Candice's mom gave me a knowing glance, like she had expected this answer all along.

And me?

I sat there, dumbfounded.

Did I question it? Absolutely not.

I wasn't about to ruin this moment by pointing out that she had just spent the past forty-eight hours actively avoiding me, emotionally destroying me, and running away from any potential relationship.

Nope.

If Candice was finally calling me her boyfriend, then guess what? I was her boyfriend.

So I did the only thing I could think of.

I reached down and took her hand.

And this time—she didn't pull away.

I sat there, holding her hand, and tried not to let my grin take over my entire face. This was real.

Her dad drove us toward our next destination—the St. George Temple.

Now, visiting the temple wasn't a new thing for me, but doing it with Candice and her entire family? That was something else entirely.

As we pulled into the parking lot, I glanced over at Candice. She wasn't pushing me away. She wasn't acting cold. In fact, for the first time since Memorial Day, she seemed . . . happy.

It was a peaceful kind of happy.

Like she had finally made a decision and was okay with it.

The Walk Around the Temple Grounds

I had always heard stories about couples visiting temple grounds and feeling the Spirit whisper to them that they were meant to be together. That kind of divine confirmation.

So as we walked onto the St. George Temple grounds, I was hopeful.

Hopeful that after everything—the cold shoulders, the months of uncertainty, the countless breakups—this would be the moment where it all finally clicked into place.

That maybe, just maybe, God would give Candice a nudge in my direction.

Candice stayed by my side the entire time.

As we continued our walk around the temple grounds, I couldn't tell you a single thing we talked about. Not because it wasn't meaningful, but because, for the first time in a long time, it wasn't about the words.

It was about her—the Candice I had fallen for.

Somewhere between the teasing comments, the light laughter, and the way she would bump into me every now and then, her playful spirit had returned. It wasn't guarded, it wasn't forced—it was just her, being herself again.

For weeks, I had been chasing after glimpses of this Candice, trying to break through the walls she had built around herself. But here, under the soft glow of the temple lights, she wasn't fighting it. She was just . . . with me.

She felt like home. It felt like everything was right in the world again. Despite everything—the breakups, the distance, the back-and-forth—Candice and I were exactly where we were supposed to be.

And maybe she was starting to feel that too.

So I let the moment breathe. I didn't push. I didn't try to define it.

I just soaked it all in.

I wasn't sure if she felt the same way, but I knew one thing—I could have walked those temple grounds with her forever.

Then, just as we started to make our way back toward the group, she turned to me—so suddenly that I barely had time to register what was happening.

And then, just like that . . .

She kissed me.

It was fast. Quick. Like she had made up her mind in a split second and just went for it before she could reconsider.

And then—just as quickly—she pulled away, gave me a look I couldn't quite decode (was that regret? pride? confusion? hunger?), and casually kept walking.

Like nothing happened.

Meanwhile, I was still standing there in the middle of the sidewalk, absolutely rocked.

Frozen.

Eyes wide.

Brain offline.

Wait. What just happened?

My system short-circuited.

Shock.

Relief.

Excitement.

Panic.

Existential dread.

And then—determination.

No way that was it.

I wasn't about to let our first kiss in years be some drive-by, blink-and-you-miss-it sneak attack that barely even qualified.

So without thinking, I caught up to her, reached for her hand, and gently pulled her back toward me—eyes locked, heart pounding—ready to go in for a real, slow, movie-worthy kiss.

And then?

BLOCKED.

She hit me with the Heisman.

Hand up. Face firm. Like, *We will* not *be doing that, thank you.*

Shut down.

Full stop.

Do not pass go. Do not collect another kiss.

I blinked, completely thrown off.

She shook her head, grinning just slightly, like she was completely in control of this situation.

Like she knew exactly how much she was torturing me.

I exhaled a quiet laugh, shaking my head in disbelief.

I had no idea what game she was playing, but one thing was certain—Candice had just kissed me on her terms.

And now, she was done.

I sighed and fell into step beside her as we made our way back to the group.

Was it the most confusing, unexpected, frustrating kiss of my life?

Absolutely.

But it was still our kiss.

The Night Before the Drive Home

After the temple kiss, I was on cloud nine.

The ride back to her aunt's house was quiet, but it wasn't uncomfortable. Candice sat close to me, her walls noticeably lower than before.

Her family, completely unaware of the emotional roller coaster that had just taken place, chatted casually as we pulled back into the driveway.

We had one more night before heading home.

Inside, her family was winding down. Her mom and dad went off to bed, and her aunt and uncle weren't far behind. The house was still, and for the first time in a long time, I was alone with Candice—no distractions, no audience.

The night air was cool, and somehow, we both ended up outside. The sky was massive, with more stars than I ever seemed to notice back in Tucson.

For the first time in a long time, there was no rush. No urgency. No forced conversation.

We just stood there.

Finally, I broke the silence.

"I don't think I've ever been this confused by a girl in my entire life."

She laughed, and it was soft—almost apologetic.

"I don't think I've ever been this confused by myself."

I turned to her, watching as she hugged her arms against the evening chill.

"Candice," I said carefully, "you don't have to have it all figured out right now. I just need to know if you want to figure it out."

She hesitated.

And then, quietly, she said, "I think I do."

That was enough for me.

We went inside, and while part of me wanted to stay up all night talking, I knew better than to push my luck. We said good night, and I went to my room—knowing that tomorrow's drive home would be another test.

I fell asleep with a strange mix of hope and exhaustion.

For the first time in two years, I felt like I wasn't chasing her anymore.

She was finally walking toward me.

The Drive Home—Nine Hours, Seven Breakups

Candice's dad tossed me the keys to her little red Saturn.

"You're driving her home," he said, a sly smile creeping across his face. "I figure you've earned it."

I laughed, but the truth was, I had no idea what I had earned. Over the last forty-eight hours, Candice had put me through every possible emotional test, and yet, here I was—still showing up, still chasing her, still convinced that somehow, she was the girl I was supposed to end up with.

Before we hit the road, Candice's dad pulled me aside one last time.

"Have you kissed her yet?"

I sighed dramatically. "Well . . . kinda. She kissed me, but it caught me off guard, so really, I didn't get to kiss her. And then she wouldn't let me kiss her again." I shook my head. "Your daughter is driving me nuts."

Her dad smirked, glanced over at Candice sitting in the other room with her mom, then . . .

"There she is, the love of your life . . . Oh, how you hate her."

I cracked up. The man was on my team.

I glanced at Candice, who was chatting with her mom, completely unaware of our conversation. She was beautiful. She was also the most confusing human I had ever met.

And now, I had nine hours alone with her in the car.

This was either going to be the best drive of my life . . . or the absolute worst.

The First Hour—The Silent Treatment

The first hour was rough.

Candice was quiet, clearly deep in thought. It was as if she had slept on everything that had happened, and instead of waking up feeling excited, she had woken up terrified.

I let her be for a while, knowing that if I pushed too hard, she'd pull away even more. I had learned that much, at least.

But I also knew one other thing: I was getting better at breaking down her walls.

So I did what I always did.

I made her laugh.

I turned up the music and sang terribly. I cracked dumb jokes. I made fun of myself. And slowly but surely, she eased up.

By the time we crossed into Nevada, she was talking to me again.

And I love to talk.

Especially when I get excited about something.

And right now? I was very excited about Candice and me.

So naturally, I started planning out the future. Nothing crazy, nothing overwhelming—just little things. When we'd see each other. What we'd do this summer. How things would work when she went back to school.

But Candice?

She wasn't a future-talker.

She wasn't a "let's map it all out right now" kind of person.

So the moment I went too far—when I started saying things that felt too real, too committed—she panicked.

And she broke up with me.

Right there, in the middle of the desert, with nowhere to escape.

"I don't know if I like you," she said suddenly.

I blinked. "Wait . . . What?"

"I just don't know," she repeated. "I think we're moving too fast."

We still had six hours left in the car together.

Not ideal timing for a breakup.

So I backed off. Made a joke. Changed the subject.

And within an hour, we were back to being a couple.

Until she broke up with me again.

This cycle repeated itself **seven times.**

Each time a little more dramatic, a little more ridiculous.

By the fourth or fifth time, I started teasing her about it.

"You know," I said, glancing at the clock, "I think it's about time for you to break up with me again. It's been almost an hour."

She rolled her eyes but smiled—and honestly, that was all I needed.

It wasn't steady.

It wasn't simple.

But somehow, it was starting to feel real.

And as chaotic as that road trip was, I wouldn't have traded it for anything.

Because ready or not,

I was falling in love with the girl who couldn't stop breaking up with me.

Chapter 17

Falling into Forever

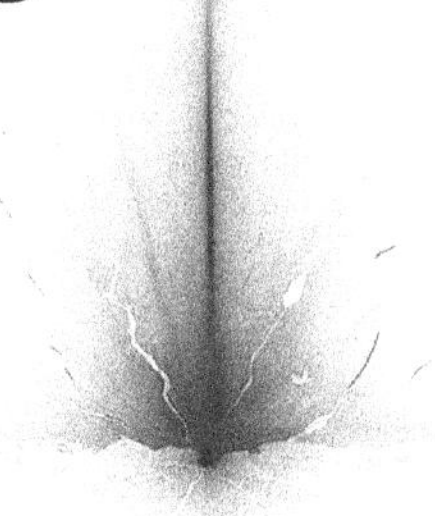

The weeks that followed our trip to St. George were a whirlwind. My life had been full of hustle—running my businesses, managing responsibilities—but suddenly, Candice was the thing I wanted to spend every free moment on.

She lived forty-five minutes away, but that didn't stop me. I would finish my work as fast as I could just to make the long drive and squeeze in every possible second with her. And she? Well, I could tell she was just as eager. The late nights, the exhaustion—we were both running on fumes, but neither of us cared.

This time, we weren't tiptoeing around what we were. We were in this.

Prayers Answered in the Most Unexpected Way

I had dated a lot. Maybe more than most guys my age. I had been engaged two times, each time thinking this might be it, only to realize, nope, this isn't it. The problem? All those girls loved the idea of me. They loved my success, my drive, the life I could offer them. But did they love me—the restless, ADD-ridden entrepreneur who had more ideas than finished projects? The guy who sometimes worked until two in the morning, then abandoned an entire business plan because he got a better idea overnight?

I wasn't so sure.

I had actually prayed about this before—prayed that when I finally found the one, I'd know she loved me, not my money or success. And honestly? I had prayed that when I got married, I'd be dirt poor—just to be sure.

Back when I had almost married someone else, I had already made my first million. I had the big house, the nice car, the financial security most guys my age could only dream of. But something felt wrong. So I tested it—I hid my money, moved back in with my parents, and waited to see what happened.

It took less than three months before the ring was shoved back in my hand.

But Candice?

Candice didn't care about any of that. She didn't care what car I drove. She didn't care where I lived. She only cared about me.

Between all our stolen hours together, we talked. A lot.

We talked about the future. About kids. About marriage. About how we'd raise a family, what mattered most to us, what we wanted our lives to look like. And with every conversation, I felt more certain— there was no part of her that I wanted to live without.

And yet, there was one looming issue.

Candice was still planning on going back to Idaho for school.

Now, there was no way I was letting her go back to BYU-Idaho. That school was famous for one thing—getting people married. There was no chance I was letting her go back and have some other guy swoop in and steal her away.

I played it cool.

"I'll do whatever's best for you," I kept telling her.

And I meant it.

But inside?

I knew the best thing for us was each other.

We started talking about marriage.

At first, it was soft and hypothetical. "If I *were* to propose, would you say yes?"

She didn't flinch.

"Yeah," she said.

That was it.

That was all I needed.

I was going to marry this girl.

Now, I just had to figure out *how*.

And first?

I needed to have a little talk with her dad.

Asking for Permission—The Costco Interrogation

Asking for a father's blessing to marry his daughter is supposed to be a big, sentimental, emotional moment.

At least, that's what I thought.

I had this whole plan in my head. I'd take Candice's dad to a nice restaurant, sit down, and have a deep, heartfelt conversation. I'd pour my soul out about how much I loved Candice, how she made me a better man, how I'd spend my life making her happy. Maybe we'd get a little misty-eyed, shake hands, and I'd leave feeling like I had just been knighted into the family.

That's how I imagined it.

What actually happened?

I got set up by two veteran cops who knew they were about to have the time of their lives at my expense.

When I called Candice's dad, Scott, I was ready to invite him to a proper sit-down dinner. Somewhere respectable. Somewhere where he wouldn't be armed.

I barely got the words out before he cut me off.

"Oh, is it that time?" he said casually, like he had been waiting for this.

I laughed nervously. "Yeah, I think so."

He didn't hesitate.

"Well, I'll be at Costco tomorrow around noon. Let's do it there."

Before I could protest, he hung up.

Costco.

Not a steakhouse. Not even a sit-down restaurant.

Costco.

A place where you can buy bulk toilet paper, a lifetime supply of peanut butter, and—apparently—a husband for your daughter.

This was not what I had in mind, but a yes was a yes, so Costco it was.

The Setup—A Scene from a Cop Show

I walked into the Costco food court at noon, expecting a casual chat with Scott.

Instead, I found two cops waiting for me.

Scott and his best friend, Tim Beam.

Now, Tim wasn't just any guy. He was practically Candice's second dad—a lifelong friend of the family, a fellow police officer, and the man who had actually rushed Candice's mom to the hospital when she was in labor.

They had strategically positioned themselves at a table right near the entrance. Not tucked away in a corner. Right in the open. Where I had to walk the full length of the food court while they watched me approach like they were about to start an interrogation.

And to top it all off?

Scott was dressed in his detective uniform, his police belt strapped around his waist—gun and badge in full view. Tim? Fully suited up in his motorcycle cop uniform.

I was walking into a full-on cop ambush.

This wasn't a meeting.

This was an initiation.

I took a deep breath and did the only logical thing I could think of.

I bought them Costco hot dogs.

As I set down their $1.25 hot dog and soda combos, Scott looked at me with a smirk.

"So . . . What's up?" he asked, as if he hadn't orchestrated this entire thing.

I cleared my throat, tried to remember all the heartfelt words I had planned, and went for it.

"I wanted to ask your permission to marry Candice."

At that moment, they both turned to each other and played a game of rock, paper, scissors.

Right in front of me.

I just sat there, watching my future being determined by a playground game.

Tim threw out scissors.

Scott threw out rock.

They both shrugged their shoulders and Scott grinned, turned back to me, and without missing a beat, said, "I guess so."

That was it.

That was my big moment.

The whole thing had lasted maybe forty-five seconds.

I had walked in expecting a deeply emotional father-to-son talk.

Instead, I got a Costco hot dog; a game of rock, paper, scissors; and a halfhearted permission slip to marry his daughter.

And honestly?

It was perfect.

These two had set me up from the start.

They had planned every detail of this moment for their own entertainment.

They knew how nervous I'd be. They knew I had been agonizing over this conversation. And instead of giving me some serious, intimidating dad speech, they had the time of their lives watching me squirm.

I left Costco feeling like I had just survived the weirdest job interview of my life.

But I had what I came for—Scott's blessing.

Now I just needed the ring.

Picking Out the Ring—A Mother's Touch

Some guys take their girlfriends to pick out the ring.

Not me.

I knew exactly what Candice wanted.

She wasn't the type who wanted something enormous and flashy. She was timeless, elegant, effortlessly beautiful. The ring had to match.

But there was no way I was doing this alone.

I called my mom.

Because if there was one person in this world who was going to make sure I didn't screw this up—it was her

My mom had been through every single one of my relationship disasters.

She had watched me fumble my way through dating, seen me get engaged (and disengaged) several times before this moment, and had been the one to say, "I told you so" every time I realized too late that I had chosen the wrong girl.

But this time?

She knew Candice was different.

She had seen the way I talked about her. The way my entire energy changed when Candice was around.

And because of that—because she knew this girl was finally the right one—she also knew that I better not screw this up with a bad ring.

So we walked into the jeweler, and that's when Mom Mode™ activated.

She went into full-on, no-nonsense, military-grade engagement ring selection mode.

"All right," she said, hands on her hips, eyes scanning every single display case like a predator looking for prey. "What are we thinking?"

I started describing the perfect ring.

"Something simple but beautiful," I said. "Something timeless. Nothing too crazy—Candice doesn't want a massive rock."

The jeweler started pulling out options.

And my mom?

She wasn't impressed.

The first ring?

"No. That's tacky."

The second ring?

"Absolutely not. That looks like something a twenty-two-year-old millionaire who doesn't actually know his girlfriend would buy."

The third ring?

"I mean . . . Do you even love this girl? Because this ring says, 'I settled.'"

I groaned, rubbing my temples. "Mom, you're killing me here."

"No, Clay," she said, looking me dead in the eye. "You've been an idiot about girls for years, but you finally found the right one. So help me, if you get this part wrong, I will never let you live it down."

She was dead serious.

She knew that this time, I had gotten the girl right.

So she was making absolutely sure that I got everything else right too.

After rejecting about fifteen different rings, I finally saw it.

A classic, timeless diamond, framed by two wedding bands lined with small, delicate diamonds—simple, elegant, and perfect.

I picked it up, turning it in my fingers, picturing Candice wearing it.

And for the first time in my entire life, I wasn't second-guessing.

No doubt. No hesitation. No *Am I really ready for this?* thoughts creeping in.

I was one hundred percent sure.

And for the first time, my mom didn't have a single critique.

She smiled.

"That's the one," she said. "You did good."

As we left the store, my mom stopped me before we got to the car.

She put both hands on my shoulders, looked me in the eye, and said,

"This time, you got it right. You got her right. And now, you got this right, too."

She was proud of me.

And honestly?

I was proud of myself, too.

Now all that was left was to actually propose.

And lucky for me—Candice's parents had just planned a trip to one of the most beautiful places on earth and invited me and her to come along.

It was time to put this ring to good use.

The Hike to Forever—Setting Up the Proposal

The fourteen-mile trek into Havasupai Falls was nothing short of breathtaking—and for once, it wasn't just the scenery making my heart race. Candice was radiant, the excitement in her eyes matching the waterfalls we had yet to see.

She was so close to me, laughing, teasing, and effortlessly making time disappear. It was like every mile hiked brought us closer, not just physically, but emotionally. I could feel it in the way she nudged me playfully, the way she looked at me when she thought I wasn't paying attention.

And that scared me.

Not because I didn't want her close—but because I knew myself. I had lived a life that would make the roughest biker gang look like a Sunday school class. A life filled with regret, bad decisions, and more repentance than most people could fathom.

But Candice?

Candice was pure.

She was as sweet and innocent as they come—a Molly Mormon through and through. The kind of girl who would blush at the simplest things, who had saved herself for marriage, who had a kind of goodness that could soften even the hardest heart.

And yet, here she was. Choosing to be close to me.

It was both humbling and terrifying.

Because for the first time in my life, I wasn't afraid of commitment—I was afraid of ruining something perfect.

So as we hiked deeper into one of the most beautiful places on earth, my mind was caught between two thoughts:

1. This is the girl I'm going to marry.

2. Don't screw this up.

I had the ring in my pack, my plan in my head, and her parents fully in on it all. But Candice?

She had no idea what was coming.

That night, as we sat around the campsite, exhausted but content, the nerves finally hit me.

Candice was completely carefree, happily chatting with her parents and soaking in the day. Meanwhile, I was mentally running through every possible scenario in my head.

What if she said no?

What if she panicked?

What if I completely botched the moment and ended up fumbling the ring into the stream?

I wanted to be confident—I really did. But the weight of the moment was real.

This wasn't just any girl. This was Candice.

The girl who had made me chase her halfway across the country. The girl who had broken up with me seven times in one car ride. The girl who had driven me to write a six-page love letter and then read it out loud in the dark like an absolute lunatic.

And somehow, after all of that, she was still here.

That night, as everyone settled into their tents, I stared up at the star-filled Arizona sky and whispered the simplest prayer:

"Please let me get this right."

Tomorrow, I was going to ask Candice to spend forever with me.

And for the first time in my life, forever didn't seem long enough.

The Proposal—Finding Forever in the Water

After lunch, Candice stretched her legs and took in the beauty of our surroundings. The canyon was unreal—like something straight out of a painting. The waterfalls, the vibrant blue-green water, the lush greenery—it was heaven on earth.

She was so happy here.

Candice had always loved exploring, hiking, and finding adventure in the simplest things. If there was a chance to go off the beaten path and do something a little different, she was all in.

So in a moment of inspiration, I said, "Hey, let's go for a walk in the river."

Her face lit up instantly.

"Yes! That sounds amazing."

Bingo.

Step one of the plan? Success.

Walking through a river sounds like a magical, peaceful experience.

And it is, if you don't mind the fact that the rocks are insanely slippery, the current is stronger than you think, and one wrong step can land you on your back, soaked, and looking like a complete fool.

But Candice?

She walked through it like she was born to do this.

Me?

I was just trying not to die.

We walked for a while, stepping carefully, holding hands to keep our balance (which, by the way, I took as another huge win). She was smiling, laughing, and completely at ease.

Meanwhile, I was in full panic mode.

Not because of the river.

But because *the* moment was coming.

I could feel the ring in my swimsuit pocket, burning a hole through the fabric.

It was time.

"Whoa," I said suddenly, stopping in my tracks.

Candice looked at me, confused.

"What?"

I pointed just ahead, pretending to spot something in the water.

"Do you see that? There's something shiny down there."

Her eyes followed my finger. I could see the curiosity spark instantly.

She loved stuff like this—hidden treasures, unexpected discoveries, anything that made an adventure feel even more special.

So, naturally, she leaned in to get a closer look.

I bent down, reached into the water, and pulled out the ring.

At first, she didn't get it.

Her brows furrowed, and she looked at me like I was insane.

"Oh no," she said, concern in her voice. "Did someone lose their ring?"

I almost laughed out loud.

I shook my head. "No, Candice."

Then, realization dawned on her face.

Her eyes flicked from the ring to my face, and I swear time froze.

By the time she looked back at me, I was already down on one knee.

I had practiced this in my head so many times—the words, the timing, the perfect moment.

But all of that disappeared.

Because the second I actually saw her face, the second I saw how much I loved her, I could barely get the words out.

Still, I took a breath and said,

"Candice . . . Will you marry me?"

Silence.

I waited.

And waited.

And . . . waited.

She just stood there.

Fingers slightly spread apart, body frozen, expression unreadable.

I started second-guessing everything.

Did I mess this up?

Did I catch her off guard too much?

Was she . . . about to say no?!

The seconds stretched painfully long.

Until finally, I had to clear my throat and remind her,

"Uh . . . You haven't answered yet."

And that's when she finally spoke.

"Uh-huh."

That was it.

That was her answer.

A barely audible, dazed, still-processing-everything uh-huh.

I decided that counted as a yes.

Before she could even fully grasp what was happening, I slipped the ring onto her finger.

It fit perfectly.

Then, the reality of it hit her.

Her body untensed. Her fingers curled around mine. And suddenly—a rush of excitement overtook her.

So when we got back to camp, Candice's first instinct was to wake up her parents.

Now, normally, waking up her parents wouldn't have been a big deal.

But her dad?

He could out-snore a grizzly bear.

You could probably hear it from the next waterfall over.

Her mom had learned long ago to just tune it out, but when Candice started shaking their tent, trying to wake them both up at once, I knew this was about to be a scene.

Her dad groaned. Her mom stirred.

Then Candice yanked the tent flap open and shoved her hand inside.

"LOOK WHAT JUST HAPPENED!"

Her dad, mid-snore, snorted awake and jerked upright.

Her mom blinked blearily at Candice, taking in the enormous grin, the flushed cheeks, the undeniable excitement.

Then, she saw the ring.

And suddenly, it was chaos.

Her mom shrieked.

Her dad laughed and pulled Candice into a hug, half asleep but clearly thrilled.

Candice kept talking a mile a minute, reliving every second of the proposal in rapid-fire detail.

Meanwhile, I stood there, watching the love of my life light up in pure joy.

And that's when I knew.

It had all been worth it.

The chasing.

The waiting.

The rejections.

The persistence.

The absolute insanity of it all.

We got married eight months later.

And I'd love to say it was a perfect, peaceful engagement full of spa days and Pinterest boards—but let's be real.

I had a past. A long one. I knew all the shortcuts, all the lines, all the ways to get what I wanted. And every time, it left me empty.

But deep down, I'd always wanted to do it differently. To honor the woman I loved. To prove I could wait.

Candice gave me that chance. She was worth honoring, worth slowing down, worth proving that no matter how many times I'd done it wrong before, I could finally do it right.

Waiting wasn't easy, but it was possible—because she was worth it. And in the end, I didn't just prove it to her. I proved it to myself: I could start fresh.

Chapter 18

What I Learned from the Chase

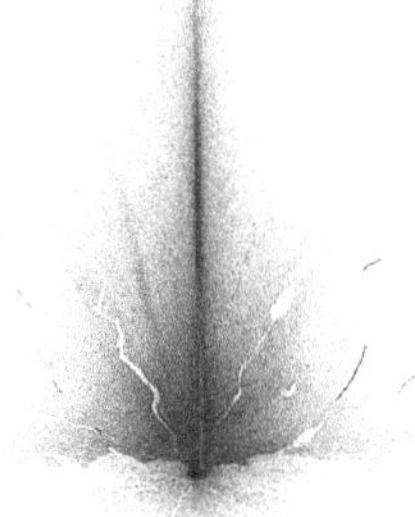

Let's get real here—when I first started chasing Candice, I didn't know I was walking into a masterclass on self-improvement taught by the most stubborn, five-foot-five professor I've ever met.

You might've thought I was just another desperate guy showing up with flowers and a six-page love letter. But I wasn't chasing Candice because I was desperate. I was chasing her because something in me knew I needed to become someone better if I ever wanted to stand a chance.

And boy, did that chase do the job.

Some of you might've been wondering, *Is this a love story or a business memoir?*

Others probably thought, *She better be something special.*

And yeah—she was. And is.

But this wasn't just a romantic chapter.

It was a turning point.

Because the chase wasn't just about her—it was about who I had to become.

Before Candice, I was great at being impressive. I knew how to sell, perform, get the deal, win the crowd. But Candice didn't care about any of that. She saw through all of it. And for once, the polished version of me—the version that usually worked—didn't work.

She didn't want a performance.

She wanted presence.

Which, in my head, went something like this:

Wait . . . the real me? Like, the "I eat cereal for dinner and doubt myself regularly" me?

Yep. That guy.

And you know what? I wasn't ready.

So I had a choice: fake it again or finally grow into someone who didn't have to.

Turns out, becoming that guy?

Way harder than I expected.

I had to stop performing.

Start digging.

Start figuring out who I was without all the noise and polish and "look at how impressive I am" energy.

There are easier ways to grow.

You could go to therapy.

Take a silent retreat.

Read a few books by people with names like "Dr. Mindful."

Me? I went full speed into emotional boot camp.

And here's what I walked out of that boot camp with:

1. Confidence isn't just a trait—it's a decision.

I had no clue if she'd say yes to anything. Not the date. Not the drive. Certainly not forever. But I kept showing up anyway. Confidence wasn't about being sure she'd love me back—it was about being sure I'd still be okay even if she didn't.

2. Communication is more than just words.

It's persistence. It's timing. It's knowing when to talk, when to listen, and when to just sit in silence. And it's learning how to be clear without being pushy—and firm without being a jerk. I wasn't always great at it, but I learned. Fast.

3. Humility will save your life.

I had to eat more humble pie during that chase than I ever thought possible. And it made me better. There's something powerful about being willing to look like a fool for something (or someone) that matters. I've done a lot of bold things in my life, but none quite like knocking on a door after a cold shoulder, hoping the answer would be different this time.

4. People don't respond to performance—they respond to presence.

I couldn't win her over with a résumé or a show. The things that made her stop and look again were the quiet moments—the real ones. The times I was just there. Unpolished. Present.

5. Becoming "marriage material" is a process—and there are easier ways to get there.

Look, if you're out there trying to be better, let me save you some time: There are much easier ways to grow than putting your heart on a spit and slow-roasting it over rejection. Life just happened to serve me the lessons this way. I wouldn't recommend it. But I'm grateful for it.

Candice didn't just challenge me—she refined me.

She wasn't impressed by what I'd built.

She was curious about who I was without it.

And that made me take a long, hard look in the mirror.

Because this wasn't about getting the girl.

This was about becoming the man.

She wasn't just a love story.

She was a mirror.

A measuring stick.

A five-foot-five spiritual growth accelerator with a cute laugh and a backbone of steel.

So if you've read this far wondering, *Why did this guy talk about Candice so much?*—this is why:

Because her presence in my life exposed the difference between who I was and who I could be.

And when she finally chose me back, I thought the hard part was over.

Turns out?

The chase was just the warm-up.

Chapter 19

The First Year of Marriage: Lessons, Loss, and a Nine-to-Five Reality Check

For Those Just Rejoining Us . . .

Welcome back.

You must be one of the readers who skipped the love story.

That's okay. I respect it.

Some people cry during *The Notebook*.

Others build spreadsheets for fun.

We all have our thing.

But just so you're not completely lost:

- I chased the girl.

- She ran.

- I ran faster.

- There were some major setbacks, some near-misses, and one homemade CD.

- And in the end? I married her.

So yes—Candice is now my wife.

And yes—if you skipped those chapters, you missed some grade-A emotional whiplash and at least three moments that probably would've made you like me more.

But I forgive you.

Because now . . . we're back.

Back to business.

Back to the grind.

Back to the part where the world doesn't care how in love you are—it just wants to know if you can deliver.

So let's get back to it.

So there I was—after everything I had done, after all the ups and downs, I had achieved what I had set out to do. The girl I wanted said yes. We had made it through the engagement, and now I had a wife, a temple marriage, and the fresh start I had always imagined. In my mind, this was the victory lap. Everything was supposed to click into place now.

Spoiler alert: It did not.

The Lingering Baggage

I had this wild idea that getting married would be like flipping a magic switch—poof!—all my past struggles gone. No more addictions, no more temptations, no more lingering bad habits. I figured once I had Candice, everything would just fix itself. But here's the thing about bad habits: They don't vanish when you say, "I do." They don't even disappear when you say, "Please forgive me." They stick around, lurking in the background, waiting for a weak moment.

Now, over time, they did fade. But it was a process, not a switch. And on top of that, I was dealing with a fresh new crisis—an identity meltdown. My last business hadn't taken off the way I envisioned, and for the first time in my life, I was faced with a terrifying reality: I needed to get a job. A real job.

Nine-to-Five vs. Ownership—The Great Debate

Candice and I came from very different worlds when it came to work. She believed in structure—forty-hour work weeks, paid vacations, 401(k)s, the whole package. Me? I believed in ownership. Making my own way. Hustling when there was work to be done and kicking back when there wasn't. The idea of someone else telling me how much my time was worth based on hours worked instead of results delivered? Absolute nightmare fuel.

I would rather work one hundred hours for free knowing I could make twenty thousand dollars than work one hundred hours with a guaranteed five thousand, because I knew I'd figure out how to turn that one hundred hours into twenty thousand dollars. And then I'd figure out how to do it in twenty-five hours.

But believing that and living with someone who saw things differently? That led to some serious growing pains. It took a full year of back-and-forth, trial-and-error, and more than a few "lively discussions" before we found a rhythm and a compromise. And by "compromise," I mostly mean me figuring out how to pretend I was okay with structure long enough to plot my escape.

My First (and Hopefully Last) Real Job

So, like a responsible adult (or at least someone trying to pretend to be one), I got a job. A real job. The kind with a set schedule, coworkers, and a boss who expected me to listen to them.

I landed a gig as a DirecTV installer, and let me tell you—it was miserable. Not because the work itself was hard. No, I could run cables and mount dishes all day. The problem? The rules. The inefficiencies. The soul-crushing realization that no one cared about improving the system.

To make things worse, I was an awful employee. I didn't know how to just do my job and shut up. I questioned everything. I tried to fix what they didn't want fixed. I made "suggestions." In hindsight, the fact that they didn't fire me sooner is impressive.

The breaking point came when I was passed over for a promotion I thought I deserved. Looking back, I get it—I wouldn't have promoted me either. But at the time? Oh, I was livid.

The Sign to Quit

I knew I had to get out, but convincing Candice was a whole other battle. Every time I brought it up, she shut it down. And honestly? I get it. We were newly married, trying to build a stable life, and here I was—already plotting my next "big idea." We hadn't even figured out how to split up laundry duty, and I was talking about jumping back into the chaos of entrepreneurship.

Then, divine intervention stepped in.

One day, my boss told me I had to start working Sundays.

Boom. That was it. The golden ticket. Even Candice—who had been adamant about me keeping the job—agreed that this was the line in the sand. I quit.

And just like that, I was back in the world of self-employment.

Now, here's what no one tells you about that moment.

The second you leave your job, *you start running out of time.*

That direct deposit you used to count on? Gone.

Health insurance? Bye.

Structure, routine, built-in purpose? You just fired all of it.

And if you don't have a nest egg—if you're jumping without a parachute—you better start selling *something* fast.

This is the part where most people get punched in the gut.

They think freedom means sleeping in and working from coffee shops.

What it actually means is this:

- **You cut your expenses to the bone.**

- **You sell everything that isn't nailed down.**

- **You figure out what you *actually* need to survive—and then you cut that in half.**

Because in the world of self-employment, cash isn't just income. It's *oxygen.*

And when it runs out, you don't go broke—you drown.

Now, look—for me, this wasn't new territory.

I'd been broke before. I'd eaten the microwave burritos. I'd had the "card declined" conversation with a straight face.

So diving back into the deep end wasn't scary.

But if this is your first time?

Buckle up, buttercup.

You're about to meet the version of yourself who can

- live on Top Ramen and optimism,

- sell half your belongings on Facebook Marketplace, and

- experience a full-blown identity crisis *before lunch.*

This isn't some romantic "follow your dreams" montage.

This is waking up at three a.m. wondering if the gas bill auto-drafted or if you're about to lose hot water *and* your pride.

Because when that steady paycheck is gone, and the clients haven't shown up yet . . .

You're not an entrepreneur.

You're an unemployed optimist with a laptop and a prayer.

So if you're reading this while sitting in a job you hate . . .

If you're fantasizing about slamming your laptop shut and walking out mid-Zoom call . . .

Just know: I support your dream.

But I also suggest you make a spreadsheet.

Because once you jump?

There's no guarantee.

No schedule.

No fallback.

Just hunger.

And hustle.

And the kind of growth you can't fake.

If you're still down for that?

Welcome to the deep end.

Lucky for me, I knew how to swim.

I landed a job as a Farmers Insurance agent, and immediately I felt like I was back in my element. Selling insurance? Piece of cake. I just used all my old tricks from selling knives, houses, or whatever else I had hustled in the past. In no time, I was one of their top agents.

Then, out of nowhere, I got a call from an old real estate client. Now, let me tell you—when you spend years handing off real estate deals to other agents, those calls disappear. Clients get comfortable working with someone else, and before you know it, they forget you even exist.

So when my phone rang and I heard, "Hey, you still doing real estate?" I nearly dropped the phone. I played it cool, obviously. "Yeah, of course," I said, as if I had been waiting for this exact moment all along. But inside? Oh, I was pumped.

I reactivated my real estate license and started handling both insurance and real estate at the same time.

And let me tell you—it was perfect. Real estate brought in those big commission checks, while insurance kept the steady, predictable income rolling in. Finally, I felt like I had cracked the code.

The Pull of Idea'l—Never Really Gone

For a while, I told myself I was done with Idea'l. I convinced myself that real estate and insurance were enough. But deep down? The itch never went away. The idea that I was meant to do something bigger was always bubbling beneath the surface.

Then, one day, a guy reached out, asking if I would teach him real estate. At first, I wasn't interested. But something about this guy made me say yes. He had nothing—no leads, no connections—but I showed him how to grind, and he took off fast.

And that's when the wheels started turning.

But I wasn't just jumping right back in. I had learned too much. I had taken my losses, my missteps, my early-timing failures, and turned them into lessons. So instead of rushing into building another empire, I focused on tailoring everything I had learned for the one guy in front of me. And then the next guy. And the next.

Because this time, I wasn't just hoping it would work—I was making sure it did.

Chapter 20

Jumping Back In: Flipping, Learning, and Making It Work

Looking back over my life, I've noticed something about people who go through the ups and downs of entrepreneurship—many of them, after a big loss, never truly jump back in. They get gun-shy. They build something, lose something, and suddenly, they're content sitting on the sidelines, sipping coffee, reminiscing about "the good old days" while convincing themselves that stability is better than risk.

I always swore I wouldn't be like that.

I made a pact with myself: No matter how many times I got knocked down, I would always get back in the game. I never wanted to be one of those guys who talked about his past successes like they were ancient history. I wanted to keep building, keep growing, keep playing the game.

One of the biggest lessons I've learned—one that I both love and hate—is this: The moment you get comfortable, your personal growth stops. If you want to grow, you have to stay uncomfortable. And let me tell you, I was getting very uncomfortable in my comfort zone.

So, naturally, life threw me a nudge.

Enter Karen (and Twenty of Her Closest Friends)

One day, I got a call from a lady who wanted to flip houses. Simple enough. She asks me to show her a couple of properties she's considering, and I say sure. I show up at the first house expecting to meet one person. Instead, people start arriving in groups.

"Oh, you must be Karen?" I ask.

"No, I'm with the group."

Another couple walks up. "Oh, so you must be Karen?"

"Nope. Just here for the tour."

At this point, I'm wondering if I'm hosting a surprise party. Then, in walks this short, firecracker of a lady, and boom—there's Karen.

Turns out, Karen had taken one of those How to Flip Houses courses from some "guru" whose business model was basically "convince people to pay thousands to learn what they could Google for free." Part of the course required students to contact a real estate agent to show them houses. Karen was the only one who actually followed through. So now I had an audience—about twenty eager students, all expecting me to drop some wisdom.

I figured, why not? I started breaking down the numbers, explaining why this first house wasn't a great flip, and answering their questions. They asked good questions—questions I had the answers to, because I had done this before. The funny thing? The so-called "guru" running the course never even showed up.

So we go to the next house. More explanations, more insights, more proof that whoever sold them that flipping course had basically scammed them. I wrapped it up by giving them one final piece of advice: "If someone's charging you a fortune to teach you how to flip houses but they've never flipped a house themselves, run."

Karen, however, stood out. She wasn't just another hopeful investor—she was actually looking to do this. So I kept her number, figuring she might be someone worth working with.

The No-Money Problem

Seeing Karen's enthusiasm got me thinking. Maybe it was time to jump back in. Maybe I needed to prove—to myself and to Candice—that real estate was still the right move.

There was just one slight issue: I had no money.

We had just bought a house. I had paid off my debts. We were stabilizing financially, but I had basically drained my savings to get there. My bank account wasn't exactly screaming *ready to invest.*

But I wasn't worried. I knew the formula. I had gone from zero to millions before, and I could do it again. The key was finding the right deal.

I started searching. And soon enough, I found the one—a solid flip with potential. I called Karen.

"Hey, I found an investment. Got it under contract. Want to partner up? I'll do all the work, you bring the money, and we split the profits fifty-fifty."

Karen was in. Or so I thought.

Then she said, "Great! I'll use a hard money lender."

Well, that's not what I expected.

See, using a hard money lender cuts into profits. We'd have to pay twelve to eighteen percent interest, plus fees. But I had found a good enough deal to make it work.

And here's the fun part—I had assumed Karen had a pile of cash sitting in the bank. Turns out, she was just really resourceful. She didn't have the money, but she knew how to get it.

Her hustle impressed me. And while using hard money wasn't ideal, it actually pushed me to start thinking about how to make things work without relying on other people's money. That lesson alone ended up shaping my next big moves.

From One Flip to a Fortune

Karen, her husband, Larry, and I moved forward. We flipped the house. Made about forty thousand dollars. Split it fifty-fifty. I also took a commission to cover my real estate fees, so I walked away in a solid position.

For Karen? This was a dream deal. She didn't put a dime of her own money in—just used her credit—and walked away with a twenty-thousand-dollar profit. That's an infinite return.

And for me? It reignited the fire.

Over the next three years, I went hard.

I flipped houses with Karen and Larry.

I flipped houses on my own.

I brought in new partners, tried new strategies, and applied every lesson I had learned—both from the wins *and* the wipeouts.

That original twenty thousand dollars?

I turned it into roughly three million dollars in real estate assets.

How?

That's a story for another day.

Actually, that would be a fun book. Stay tuned for:

Don't Kick the Crackheads Out Too Early.

(If you know, you know.)

But this chapter?

This one was about something else entirely:

Momentum.

Because when life hits hard, the instinct is to pause.

To freeze.

To overthink.

But I've learned something about momentum—

it doesn't wait for clarity.

You don't need a perfect plan.

You need a push.

Even a messy one.

Once I jumped back in, the energy started building again.

I didn't have everything figured out—but I didn't need to.

Because progress compounds.

And movement creates more movement.

It's like catching a wave:

You paddle like crazy, not because it's graceful . . .

but because if you don't, you miss it.

This wasn't about brilliance.

It was about staying in motion long enough to ride something bigger than me.

And this phase?

This was the setup for everything that came next.

It reconnected me with the right people.

It put me in the right rooms.

And most importantly, it reminded me that no matter how many times I had to start over . . .

I *knew* how to rise again.

Because setbacks aren't the end.

They're just part of the ride.

The Real Estate Cheat Code

Let's be real—real estate can be overwhelming. People love to complicate it with fancy jargon, market speculation, and spreadsheets that look like they belong at NASA. But at the end of the day, making money in real estate isn't magic. It's about knowing a few solid rules and actually sticking to them.

I've learned these rules the hard way—by missing out on deals I should have jumped on, by watching others crash and burn on bad flips, and by seeing firsthand how emotion can make people overpay for a house just because they "felt something" when they walked through the front door. If you read the chapter about my first flip, you know I learned a lot from that experience. I made money, but I also saw exactly how things could have gone wrong. That deal shaped the way I approached every deal after it.

So instead of writing a never-ending manual on every little detail, I'm giving you the three rules that have made me money, saved me from disasters, and kept me from losing sleep at night.

Rule #1: Be Patient . . .
but Ready to Buy in Five Seconds

This sounds like a contradiction, but stick with me.

- Be patient when looking for a house. Don't get desperate. Whether it's for your family or an investment, taking whatever is available because you're in a hurry is how people get stuck with overpriced dumps.

- But when you find the right house, don't hesitate. The second you find "the one," assume five other people just had the same revelation. If you wait until morning to pray about it, someone else already wrote the offer.

How I Learned This the Hard Way

When I was new, I had tons of clients say, "We love it, but we need to sleep on it." I'd nod and say, "Of course, take your time." By morning? Gone. Every. Single. Time. After watching this happen enough, I started warning clients up front: If you have to pray, pray now. Once we're out there looking, we're making decisions.

And guess what? We never lost another house.

The same rule applies to investments. The deals I didn't pull the trigger on? I still think about them. I drive by those properties and get that deep, soul-crushing regret. I've lost too many great deals by hesitating. And I refuse to let it happen again.

Rule #2: Make Sure It's Worth What You're Paying

The worst way to lose money in real estate? Overpaying. Here's how to avoid that mistake:

- Primary residence: Treat it like an investment. Most people think they're buying their "forever home." They're wrong. The average American moves twelve times in their life. Buy a house you can sell later without losing money. And don't get emotional. We all know Tiny Tim is going to grow up there, but only for a few years. You don't get emotional over the apartment you rented for five years, so don't do it here—unless you're forty, bought four other houses, and have your life established.

- Rental properties: My rule is simple: If the mortgage payment is a thousand dollars, the rent must be at least thirteen hundred. If I can't clear three hundred dollars above the mortgage, I don't buy it. That cushion covers property mortgage and leaves room for maintenance.

- Flipping houses: Flipping is not for beginners. It's a business, not a fun weekend project. My rule? Find the worst house in a great neighborhood. After all costs (purchase, renovation, commissions, and concessions), I need to walk away with at least twenty thousand dollars in profit—or I don't buy it.

Why This Rule Saves You

HGTV has created some of the best deals of my life. Seriously. People watch a few episodes, think they're flippers, then overspend on a renovation. By the time they realize they're in too deep, they need to dump the property—at a loss. That's where I come in, buying their mistake at a discount.

I once saw a guy spend seventy-five thousand dollars on a flip thinking he'd make a fortune. He turned a two-hundred-thousand-dollar house into a two-hundred-thousand-dollar house . . . with nicer floors. He sold at a loss. Why? Because he broke the rule: Don't overpay, and don't over-renovate.

Rule #3: Always Buy with the Long-Term in Mind

I don't care what's happening in the market today. I buy real estate with a five- to seven-year mindset. If everything goes south, I need to be able to hold on to that property until things bounce back.

- Flipping? I make sure I can turn it into a rental if needed. If the market crashes mid-project, I'll rent it out and wait.

- Rentals? I never touch the profits. They build up for future repairs and maintenance. Also, if I'm tight on cash, I get a home warranty for the first couple of years—just in case.

- Unexpected costs? Happens all the time. You tear down a wall and find a plumbing disaster. If you can't afford to hold on to a property when things go sideways, you're setting yourself up for failure.

How This Mindset Saved Me

I've had flips where unexpected problems pushed the budget too far. Instead of taking a loss, I turned them into rentals. A few years later, I sold them at a huge profit. If I had been in a rush to cash out, I would have lost money. Instead, I made money tomorrow and the following year.

That's the thing about real estate. It's not just about flipping houses—it's about thinking bigger. I never wanted to be just another house flipper. I wasn't the biggest flipper in the world, and I didn't want to be. Instead, I focused on helping people get into the business, even if that meant creating my own competition. A lot of those flippers I helped get started are still in the business today, pulling in six figures or more years later. Meanwhile, I took what I learned and built something bigger.

Final Thoughts: Stick to the Rules, Ignore the Noise

These three rules have worked for me over and over again. If you buy with a long-term mindset, don't overpay, and act fast when it matters—you'll win. Simple as that.

Don't overcomplicate it. Stick to the math, stay patient, and when the right deal shows up—jump.

The secret to real estate is simple: Buy smart, buy fast, and don't let HGTV ruin your life. Now, go find your deal and don't hesitate—or I'll be the one buying it instead.

And yes, I know—**location matters.** It's the golden rule in real estate. A great location can boost your returns, no doubt. A great house in the wrong situation isn't an asset. It's a money pit with nice views and a slow death grip on your sanity.

I knew how to avoid those mistakes.

Because at this point in my career, I wasn't just making money—I was making momentum.

Real estate was working.

Insurance was working.

The businesses were growing.

I had a team, a rhythm, a system.

But one part of the machine kept jamming.

One part never seemed to run right.

No matter how smart I played it, how hard I worked, or how much I delegated—**construction** was always the anchor. Dragging behind. Bleeding money. Costing me time, deals, and sleep.

And it wasn't just annoying anymore.

It was *personal.*

Chapter 22

Screw It.
I'll Build My Own School

Let me be honest:

I was done.

Not just "had a rough day" done. I mean *truly* done—mentally, emotionally, and drywall-dust-on-your-face exhausted.

It was July.

The air was thick.

I was managing a crew mid-renovation when one of the guys texted me:

"Bro, I can't. Sry."

That was it.

No follow-up. No context. Just a grown man tapping out of a job via text.

But honestly? That wasn't even the worst part.

A few months earlier, my best guy—my rock, my most skilled, most reliable builder—broke his back on the job.

He was the kind of worker every contractor dreams about.

One guy. No drama. No supervision. Just solid, consistent output and decades of quiet competence.

After the injury, I tried to replace him.

Not with one guy.

Not even two.

I hired **four** people to fill his role.

And somehow, *all four of them together* still couldn't do what he used to do in a single day.

They weren't lazy. They weren't bad people.

They were just . . . unprepared.

And that's when it hit me:

We didn't have a labor shortage.

We had a training collapse.

What Happened to the Builders?

We spent decades telling young people:

"If you don't go to college, you'll be flipping burgers for the rest of your life."

But we forgot to mention that flipping houses pays better—and requires an actual skill set.

So we cut shop class.

We shut down woodshops and auto bays.

We stripped hands-on learning from schools and replaced it with test prep, screen time, and lectures.

We trained kids to memorize, not master.

To watch, not *do.*

And now, the few people who still know how to build?

They're aging out.

Retiring. Disappearing.

And we're looking around like, *Why can't anyone frame a wall anymore?*

We know why.

We just don't want to admit we let it happen.

I Tried to Fix It the Conventional Way

Before you think I jumped straight to "build a school," trust me—I tried everything else.

I ran paid apprenticeships.

They fell apart.

I tested on-site training programs.

Total chaos.

I hired "experienced" workers who showed up with tool belts and no clue. One guy literally asked me how to use a tape measure.

A tape measure.

What I learned is this:

Throwing someone into a job site and hoping they absorb the skills through exposure is not training.

It's gambling.

And in construction, gambling is expensive.

The old-school method of "learn by doing" only works if someone's there to teach—and if there's time to actually *repeat* the skill until it sticks.

That's not how job sites work anymore.

They're under pressure. Fast-moving.

You don't get five tries to fix your mistake—you get one.

So unless you're already skilled, you're in the way.

The Training System Wasn't Broken— It Was Missing

Here's what real training takes:

- **Repetition.** Mastery doesn't come from watching—it comes from doing it over and over.

- **Consistency.** Five days a week, like a job. Not "whenever someone's free."

- **Focus.** One skill at a time. Not framing Monday, HVAC Tuesday, and tile work by Friday.

- **Buy-in.** If people don't have skin in the game, they won't push through the hard parts.

I kept looking for a company or program that was doing this.

Something structured. Repeatable. Scalable.

Nothing.

There were schools that *claimed* to teach the trades—but the students barely touched tools. They spent most of their time in classrooms, reading about how other people build things.

We didn't need more lectures.

We needed a **factory for builders.**

A controlled environment where people could mess up safely, try again, and walk away with actual competence—not a just certificate.

So . . . I Built It

I didn't want to start a school.

That wasn't the plan.

But when you've run out of excuses, and you keep seeing the same problem show up in every job, every industry, every young person who walks through the door . . .

Eventually, you stop waiting for someone else to fix it.

You roll up your sleeves and do it yourself.

That's how Idea'l started.

Not as a business strategy.

Not because I thought education reform would be fun.

But because I knew if we didn't build something better—**we were going to lose an entire generation of builders.**

And not just in construction.

In everything.

Because if you can't build a house, you can't build a school, or a hospital, or a church.

And if you can't train someone how to build . . .

Then eventually, you won't have a society worth living in.

So yeah. I built a school.

A real one.

With tools, real projects, and a schedule that looks more like a job site than a lecture hall.

We don't just teach people how to build homes.

We teach them how to build lives.

Chapter 23

The Battle Between "Not Qualified" and "Most Qualified"

Knowing you should do something and actually doing it are two completely different things.

Add in the feeling that you're totally unqualified to even try, and your brain will start running laps around itself.

That's where I was—stuck in a mental loop of waiting, doubting, hoping . . . and slowly realizing:

No one else is coming.

For years, I held out hope that someone else would do what I knew needed to be done. I spent almost two decades learning the ins and outs of business, real estate, and construction—not just to build wealth, but to prepare. I was waiting for someone to step up and fix the broken education system, to address the skilled labor shortage, to do the thing I could clearly see needed doing.

But no one did.

By year ten, the cracks weren't cracks anymore. They were craters.

Universities were collecting tuition checks but graduating students with no real skills.

Trade knowledge was disappearing.

The system wasn't just broken—it was devouring entire generations. And the longer I waited, the more obvious it became:

If it was going to happen, it had to be me.

What really cemented it was when I started hearing people on TV say things I'd been shouting for fifteen years—word for word. These were the same ideas that once got me laughed out of boardrooms, and now they were being treated like groundbreaking revelations.

That's when I knew:

I wasn't crazy.

I was early.

And suddenly, people were agreeing with me. I'd start explaining the model and they'd nod like it was the most obvious thing in the world. And I thought, *Where were you when I was getting roasted for this in 2005?*

But even with the validation, the doubt crept in.

I wasn't a professor.

I didn't have a degree in educational theory.

I didn't wear tweed or have a bookshelf full of academic credentials.

I was just . . . me. A guy who'd built companies from scratch. Who had trained people, hired people, lost people. A guy who had watched traditional education fail people he loved. A guy who knew, deep in his gut, that **we could do this better.**

And the weird thing was, I felt both wildly underqualified . . . and like the **most qualified person in the world** to do this.

Because I'd *lived it.*

I didn't learn from textbooks—I learned from risk. From failure. From trying to teach people with no confidence, no structure, and no road map. And through all of it, I never stopped learning.

Still, the mental battle didn't go away.

One minute I'd think, *This will cost everything you've built.*

The next, *You're more prepared than anyone else on the planet.*

So I kept studying.

Not surface-level stuff—I went deep. Research, data, case studies. I didn't just want to complain about the problem. I wanted to *solve* it.

And the more I studied, the more I realized—I wasn't wrong. I was just ahead of the curve.

If I ever doubted myself, Candice would shut it down instantly. She believed in me in a way I couldn't always believe in myself. She'd say, "You always figure it out. You always do what you say you're going to do."

And she was right.

Not because I'm the smartest.

But because I'm relentless.

I'm not great at everything. But I don't quit. Ever.

And this?

This was going to demand **every ounce of growth I had left in me.**

What's funny is . . . everyone else saw it coming before I did.

People around me knew I was going to build the school before I said it out loud.

And when I finally committed?

No one doubted me. Not anymore.

That was almost disappointing.

Because sometimes, other people's doubt is what fuels you. And when nobody's doubting you, you have to dig deep and find the fire for yourself.

And I did.

Because once I committed, the fear didn't go away—but it lost its power.

That was the moment Idea'l was reborn.

Not as an experiment.

Not as a someday dream.

But as a **mission.**

No degree.

No polished pedigree.

No perfect road map.

Just the right experience, the right vision, and the willingness to take the hit if it didn't work.

I wasn't looking for someone else to lead it anymore.

I was going to build it myself.

And if I failed?

Well . . . at least I wouldn't be just another guy sitting around, waiting for someone else to fix it.

Besides, worst case? I crash and burn and walk away with a great story.

And let's be honest—most success stories *start* with a disaster anyway.

Might as well make it a good one.

So there I was: underqualified, overconfident, and fully committed.

What could possibly go wrong?

(Answer: Everything. But that's what makes it fun.)

Chapter 24
Education That Actually Works

At its core, Idea'l isn't just a business.

It's a mission.

I believe people were designed to create—to build, to solve problems, to contribute.

Work isn't just about money. It's about purpose.

And when people work with their hands—when they build something real—they experience a kind of fulfillment that no amount of classroom lectures can replicate.

Honestly, some of the best life lessons come from smashing your thumb with a hammer and realizing, yes, you really should've paid attention.

From a deeper perspective—call it philosophical, call it theological—I believe work is fundamental to who we are.

Every civilization that has thrived . . . did so through craftsmanship, creativity, and hands-on ingenuity.

Building isn't just a job skill.

It's part of our design.

Strip that away, and you don't just lose productivity—you lose identity.

You create generations that feel aimless, disconnected, unsure of their place in the world.

And the more passive our learning has become, the more that void has grown.

Modern education doesn't build purpose.

It builds compliance.

It teaches people to memorize, not to master.

Instead of developing potential, we've created a pipeline that produces debt, degrees, and disappointment.

And this isn't just an individual problem.

It's societal.

Because when a nation stops valuing the trades, it stops investing in its own survival.

If nobody knows how to build, maintain, or fix things . . . well, good luck running hospitals, data centers, or *bathrooms that work.*

We're already halfway there.

If you've ever seen a twenty-year-old try to change a tire—or give up entirely—you know what I'm talking about.

So when I rebuilt Idea'l, I wasn't just thinking about a school.

I was thinking about a **reclamation**—a recovery of something we've lost:

Purpose through work.

Confidence through skill.

Fulfillment through *doing.*

The Idea'l Model—The Environment Is the Teacher

Idea'l isn't a trade school with better branding.

It's a complete reimagining of what education *should* be.

We built a system where the **environment** teaches the student.

Where mistakes are allowed—expected, even—and where every error is a lesson in disguise.

• The Environment Is the Teacher

No lectures. No droning professors.

We build real environments where the *work itself* provides the feedback.

A crooked door teaches alignment.

A busted drywall seam teaches patience.

The lesson is built into the process—so students *learn by doing,* not listening.

• People Learn Faster When Reality Corrects Them

When the wall is crooked, you don't need a lecture to know something's wrong.

You *see* it.

You *feel* it.

You *fix* it.

That's education.

You haven't truly learned precision until you cut the same board wrong three times and finally get it right. You haven't understood humility until you over-mud drywall and spend three hours sanding your pride off the wall.

Reality teaches without ego.

And students listen—because it's their own work talking back.

• No Pushback. Just Pure Learning.

When a teacher tells you something, you might roll your eyes.

When *reality* tells you?

You unfortunately have to believe it.

This eliminates friction. No arguing. No theory battles. Just action → consequence → growth.

And that's where true mastery begins.

• Seamless Transition into the Workforce

At Idea'l, there's no "graduation day panic."

There's no awkward leap from classroom to career.

Our students have already worked real shifts, solved real problems, and delivered real outcomes.

By the time they finish?

They're not "looking for experience."

They *have* it.

They're not guessing if they can do the job—they've *already done it.*

+ **A Self-Sustaining System**

Most schools require constant intervention just to keep students moving.

At Idea'l, the system trains itself.

Because when the environment is built right—

it doesn't just teach.

It scales.

As we grow, we don't dilute the experience. We multiply it.

Every project is another classroom.

Every student becomes another mentor.

The system evolves—but the results stay real.

Why Traditional Education Can't Compete

The current model trains students to sit still, follow rules, take tests, and collect debt.

It doesn't train them to *win.*

It convinces them that the only path to success runs through a four-year university, where they'll spend thousands of dollars studying things that have no connection to the real world.

And when they graduate?

When they realize no one's hiring them for their twenty-eight-page sociology paper on gender dynamics in medieval France?

They're told it's *their* fault.

They didn't network enough.

They didn't hustle hard enough.

They didn't believe in themselves.

What a joke.

Meanwhile, companies are begging for plumbers.

Electricians. Welders. Machinists. Construction managers.

Actual jobs.

With actual demand.

And *actual paychecks.*

Our goal isn't just to teach trades.

It's to rebuild *confidence.*

To remind people that they're not broken.

The system is.

Imagine a world where education actually led to results.

Where people finished school and immediately stepped into careers.

Where success didn't require debt, detours, or "waiting your turn."

This wasn't some stroke of genius.

It was sixteen years of bleeding, building, failing, fixing, and—honestly—understanding what God had been trying to teach me all along.

This isn't just about skills.

It's about restoring a system that should've never been broken.

And if that means breaking a few rules along the way?

Well . . .

Those rules were probably written by the same people who think you need one hundred thousand dollars to learn how to communicate in a group setting.

We'll be fine.

Chapter 25

The Science Behind the Model

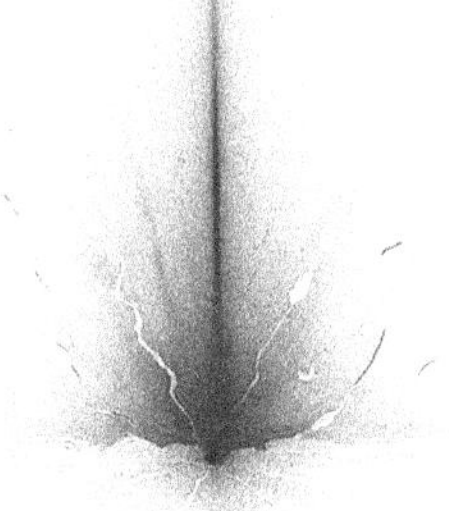

It was 2021.

I was already running multiple businesses and had every reason to focus on the work in front of me.

But I couldn't shake it.

Something kept pulling me back to education. To the gap I'd seen firsthand for years.

So I started digging. Really digging.

And what I found hit me like a freight train.

Study after study confirmed everything I'd been saying for years.

The stuff people used to roll their eyes at?

Now it was backed by hard data from Harvard, psychology journals, and decades of research.

It was no longer a hunch.

That's when I knew: I couldn't ignore it anymore.

I had to build this.

What follows is the science that stopped me in my tracks—
and launched the next chapter of my life.

Active Learning—Engaging the Mind
(Because Sitting and Listening Isn't Learning)

- **Harvard University**[1] found that students in active learning environments significantly outperformed those in traditional lecture settings—even though they *felt* like they were learning less.

That's huge.

Because one of the biggest lies in education is this:

"If it feels easy, it must be working."

Nope.

Harvard's research proves the opposite: When students feel too comfortable, they're usually not learning anything.

Let's break it down:

- You sit through a lecture, nodding along like a genius.

- You leave feeling confident.

- Two days later . . . *gone.* Like it never happened.

Meanwhile, students in interactive environments—solving problems, working with their hands, making mistakes—feel challenged. Frustrated, even.

But their **retention skyrockets.**

When you're doing the work, your brain is forced to engage.

It makes decisions. It connects dots. It *learns.*

What this meant to me:

If Harvard says "get up and do something" beats "sit and listen,"

then I was right again and would continue to build around these exact principles.

No lectures. No fluff. Just action → feedback → mastery.

Experiential Learning—
Why the Real World Teaches Better Than
Any Textbook

- Extensive research[2] found that experiential learning doesn't just improve academic performance. It also increases empathy, social behavior, and well-being.

In other words:

Doing stuff makes you smarter—and a better human.

Let's compare:

- **Student A** takes notes on teamwork, leadership, and communication.

- **Student B** leads a team under pressure, works through real conflicts, and adapts on the fly.

Who's more prepared for life?

The answer's obvious.

Experience doesn't just teach skills.

It forms identity.

What this meant to me:

I didn't want students who could *describe* leadership.

I wanted students who had led.

Who had failed.

Who had learned to stand up again with calloused hands and a clear head.

Because no textbook prepares you for drywall that won't dry, or a partner who quits mid-project.

Real leadership happens in *real* conditions.

Retention Through Active Learning
(Or Why Sitting in a Chair Doesn't Equal Learning)

- Studies[3] have confirmed that **students in active learning environments retained more information and performed better across the board.**

Let's make it stupid simple:

- Listen passively? You forget.

- You **do** something? You remember.

Traditional education is like trying to send a text with a rotary phone.

We know there's a better way—but we keep spinning the dial.
What this meant to me:
We weren't going to "deliver information."
We were going to build **retention machines.**

- No passive lectures.

- No memorization for a test.

- No forgetting what you learned—because you *used* it.

It's not magic.
It's neuroscience.

The Science of Multimodal Learning
(Or Why Sitting in Rows Is Dumb)

Let's be honest—we've all sat in classrooms where time stopped moving.

Traditional schools love the "lecture, notes, test" format.
But research? Not so much.

- **Dual Coding Theory:**[4] We retain more when we combine visuals and spoken words. Two brain pathways. Double the recall.

- Pairing images with audio explanations deepens learning better than text alone.[5]

- Multisensory learning is faster, more effective, and longer lasting.[6]

Even the VARK model (visual, auditory, kinesthetic) stumbled onto something useful: **Most people don't have a "type"—they learn best when all their senses are involved.**

Translation?

Reading a book on plumbing ≠ learning plumbing.

You learn when your hands are wet, the pipe is leaking, and you *fix it.*

What this meant to me:

If we could show it instead of explain it—we'd show it.

If we could practice it instead of lecturing about it—we'd practice it.

We were done with passive learning.

We were building a multisensory, multimodal experience that made information **stick.**

Why Your Brain Loves Pictures

- Frank Dwyer showed that combining visuals with instruction leads to **better retention, faster learning, and higher confidence.**[7]

Your brain was made for images and motion.

Not bullet points and boredom.

Be honest:

Would you rather . . .

1. Read about how an engine works?

2. Or pull one apart—bolt by bolt—and feel the timing chain in your hand?

Because let's be real:

You don't *learn* an engine by reading about it.

You learn it by busting your knuckles.

By getting grease on your jeans and realizing—*oh, that's what torque feels like.*

But school doesn't teach like that.

It teaches by distance.

By sitting, watching, memorizing, forgetting.

Because reading is safe.

Passive. Clean.

But the brain doesn't retain clean.

We retain what we wrestle with.

What we bleed on.

What we build.

That's why:

- Students wire real circuits.

- Frame real walls.

- Build from real blueprints—and see what happens when they mess up.

Learning doesn't stick because it's clean.

It sticks because it's real.

The Military Got It Right

- During World War II, US Army trainers discovered what educators still see today: **People learn best by doing.** Soldiers didn't get good at shooting by reading manuals. They got good by firing under pressure—again and again—until the skill stuck.

That shift became the backbone of US military training. By the end of the war, hands-on, field-based drills had largely replaced classroom lectures. It wasn't theoretical. It was a practical lesson taught by necessity: **Realistic practice builds real skill.**

The story stuck. Later education researchers traced modern learning theories back to this moment in history—especially wartime training programs at the Army's Ordnance School in Aberdeen, Maryland. Although the original data has been lost, the impact remains: **"Learning by doing" became the gold standard not only for the battlefield but also for all skill-building environments.**[8]

You don't learn project management from a slideshow. You learn it when five people need direction, the schedule's off, and someone just installed the wrong window.

What this meant to me:

We weren't waiting for students to "get ready." We were throwing them in—safely—and letting the work shape them. Because fast, real feedback builds faster, real skill.

The Power of Perceptual Learning

- Eleanor Gibson showed that humans learn best by doing the same task over and over—until it becomes second nature.[9]

This is how experts are built.

A good electrician doesn't have to pause and think through every step—they've wired so many panels that their hands already know what to do.

A seasoned nurse spots complications before the monitors do.

A good builder can *feel* when the framing's off.

That's perceptual learning.

It's instinct built from repetition.

What this meant to me:

We weren't just building competence.

We were building **confidence.**

Our students:

- Don't just study electrical—they install it, test it, and trouble-shoot it.

- Don't just read blueprints—they *build* from them.

- Don't just role-play leadership—they run real teams with real consequences.

Because real skill isn't taught.

It's trained.

Final Thoughts:
Built on Research, Not Tradition

Harvard. Psychology journals. Military studies. Cognitive science.

They all say the same things:

- Active learning works.

- Multimodal learning accelerates retention.

- Hands-on experience creates real skill and real confidence.

So why is traditional education still clinging to lectures, tests, and textbook trivia?

Because it's easy. It's predictable. And it's profitable

It wasn't built to help students—it was built to keep the system moving.

But I wasn't interested in "keeping things moving."

I was interested in building something that **works.**

Something that prepares people for **life,** not just for Scantrons.

Something that creates:

- Confident workers

- Capable leaders

- Real people who solve real problems

From Research to Reality

This research didn't surprise me.

It confirmed what I had already lived—through years of building businesses, training people, and watching systems fail.

It gave me the *why* behind what I had already seen.

But knowing something and building it?

That's where it gets real.

Because now I had the data, the fire, and the vision.

What I didn't have?

A blueprint.

A budget.

A clue how I was going to pull this off.

But I knew one thing for sure:

It had to be done.

And somehow . . .

I was going to figure it out.

Chapter 26

Look at My Son

On paper, life looked perfect.

I was making a fortune in real estate and insurance. I had freedom, financial security, beautiful things. I could walk away from work midweek, take a trip, spoil my wife, give to good causes, and still watch the money roll in.

And for once—I wasn't chasing anything new.

I wasn't building, pushing, solving.

I was just . . . coasting.

But deep down, I wasn't at peace.

Because the vision for the Idea'l wouldn't shut up.

I had just finished poring over all the research—decades of data that basically screamed, *Hey, genius, you were right.*

The stuff people laughed at when I first said it? The ideas they dismissed as naive or impossible?

Now Harvard, Stanford, the military, cognitive science—they were all publishing studies confirming exactly what I'd been shouting for years.

It should have felt like a win.

Instead, it felt like a burden.

Because now I couldn't unsee it.

If we didn't build something different—something real—we weren't just heading for a skills gap.

We were heading for a collapse.

And suddenly, I had a choice.

Walk away, pretend I didn't see it.

Or lean in—and risk everything.

That's when the panic hit.

This wasn't a house flip.

This wasn't a commission-based startup with a three-month launch runway.

This was *massive.*

National. Scalable. Generational.

And I knew how hard it would be.

Not the fake kind of hard people post about on LinkedIn.

I'm talking "this could break me—financially, mentally, emotionally" kind of hard.

So I did the only thing that made sense in a moment like that.

I hit my knees.

Literally.

It wasn't even dramatic.

It was quiet. Personal.

Exhausted.

I remember kneeling there, elbows on the bed, face in my hands, whispering, "God . . . are You sure about this?"

Because here's the truth: I'm not the guy you'd pick for this on paper.

"God, I'm great at real estate. I'm great at insurance. I can even teach a mean ballroom class, which I feel like should count for something. But start a national trades education revolution? Are You *sure* You don't want someone with, I don't know . . . a PhD?"

I stayed there for a while.

No agenda. No prayer formula.

Just a man in his thirties, with everything to lose, asking Heaven if he was supposed to throw it all on the line.

And then I heard it.

Just one sentence.

"Look at My Son."

That's all.

No road map. No angelic voice. Just five words that hit me so deeply I almost laughed.

"Look at My Son."

Classic God.

Total identity crisis? Life-altering decision? Existential prayer?

Five words.

No follow-up.

So I sat with it.

I wanted more. But that's all I got.

So I started doing the only thing I could: I looked.

And what I saw changed everything.

Jesus Started in Construction

Before Jesus ever taught a parable . . .

Before He performed a miracle . . .

Before anyone called Him Rabbi, Messiah, or Savior . . .

He was a builder.

Not metaphorically.

Not symbolically.

Literally.

He worked with His hands.

He showed up early. Carried wood. Hauled stone.

Measured. Cut. Shaped. Sanded. Fixed.

He knew splinters and sweat and the ache of tired muscles.

God could have placed His Son anywhere:

- In the temple, learning law

- In the palace, studying governance

- In the synagogue, debating scripture

But He didn't.

He put Him in a workshop.

Jesus learned in the dust—by doing.

He built with Joseph. Repaired tools. Took orders. Dealt with customers. Made things better with His hands.

He lived the exact kind of life modern society now calls a "fallback plan."

And it wasn't a mistake.

It was a *model*.

God could've trained Jesus through scholars. Instead, He chose *structure* and *substance*.

The trade was part of the training.

Because what do the trades teach?

- **Patience**—You don't rush a cut. You don't skip the prep work.

- **Endurance**—You finish the job, even if it rains or your back's shot.

- **Creativity**—Every broken thing is a puzzle.

- **Service**—Real value is built when you solve someone else's need.

- **Discipline**—Good work takes time. Great work takes practice.

- **Humility**—You make mistakes. You own them. Then you fix them.

The workshop was Jesus' first classroom.

And the world was His final project.

So if construction was good enough for the Son of God—

it's good enough for every kid who's ever been told he's not smart because he didn't test well.

We've Forgotten What's Sacred

Fast-forward to now.

We've built an education system that treats trades as second-class.

We tell students that if they're not "college material," maybe they can settle for a career in construction.

As if building something from scratch is less valuable than memorizing facts you'll forget by spring break.

We rank SAT scores over skill.

We glorify cubicles and condemn callouses.

We worship credentials and ignore competence.

And then we act confused when:

- Kids have no confidence

- Workers don't show up

- No one wants to fix what's broken

We call it a "labor shortage," like it's just some mysterious economic trend.

It's not mysterious.

We created it.

One guidance counselor speech at a time.

One job fair at a time.

One subtle shrug when a student says, "I think I'd rather work with my hands."

All while forgetting that the Son of God spent most of His life holding a hammer.

This Work Is Holy

The more I thought about it, the more I realized:

This isn't just about fixing education.

It's about reclaiming something sacred.

Because creating . . . fixing . . . building . . .

That's God's work.

He could've called Himself the Great Lecturer, the Divine Theorist, the Master Administrator.

But He chose to introduce Himself with a different title:

Creator.

He formed.

He shaped.

He breathed life into dust.

That's not just theology.

That's identity.

Which means building things—real, tangible things—*reflects the nature of God.*

That was the moment I stopped asking, "Why me?"

And started asking, "Okay . . . How do I begin?"

I didn't have a business plan.

I didn't have the money.

But I had a conviction.

So I did what I always do.

I got to work.

I started writing a curriculum.

Started sketching houses.

But mostly? I started designing the **environment.**

A place where people could show up.

Make mistakes.

Fix them.

Try again.

And leave more capable, more confident, and more whole than when they arrived.

It wasn't perfect.

It wasn't polished.

It wasn't even fully planned.

But it was **real.**

And for once, that was enough to begin.

Still Standing

Here's what I can tell you—because we're still in the thick of it: We found a way. We always do.

Even with the roadblocks.

Even with the licensing nightmares.

Even with the money wiped out and the momentum dragged to a halt . . .

We kept building.

And now?

We're proudly serving Native American communities, delivering in Utah, and reaching into every corner of Arizona.

Not because it was easy.

Not because we had special connections.

But because we refuse to quit.

And this?

This is just the start.

Because we're not done until every community has access to real training, real opportunity, and real homes built by the people who live there.

We're not just building houses—we're building hope, skill by skill, town by town.

So if we haven't made it to your neighborhood yet . . .

Hang tight.

We're on our way.
We're not going anywhere.
Not now. Not ever.
We're here to stay.

Chapter 27

Shut Down, Set Back, Still Standing

When you start something new—*truly* new—something no one's ever actually done, only theorized about, you expect chaos.

Because that's what innovation looks like up close.

It's loud. Unpolished. Uncomfortable.

It doesn't follow blueprints.

It *makes* them.

But if you know it's going to be chaotic—

if you expect the mess—

then it's not really chaos.

It's momentum in disguise.

So no—we weren't stumbling into this blind.

This wasn't some last-minute scramble.

A tight crew of builders, educators, and real-world doers,

huddled around a scratched-up table—blueprints in one hand, burritos in the other—asking the kind of question most schools would never dare to ask:

"What if we could train someone faster, better, and cheaper—without ever opening a textbook?"

We didn't have it all figured out.

But we had the right instincts.

And the right people.

And that was enough to start.

We weren't checking boxes.

We were flipping the system.

One question at a time.

"If this works, we've got a revolution."

"If it doesn't? At least we'll fail loudly enough to make someone else fix it."

And then we asked the real question:

"Can we teach twenty completely different people—each with their own wiring, baggage, and brilliance—without dumbing it down, splitting it up, or teaching twenty separate lessons?"

Not by standing over them.

Not by micromanaging every move.

Not by pretending learning happens when someone else does all the thinking for you.

Because one-on-one teaching isn't the gold standard.

Freedom is.

Pressure is.

Time to wrestle with something real—*that's* where growth lives.

We weren't trying to spoon-feed answers.

We were trying to create a space where people could push themselves—hard.

A system that gave them just enough structure to stay focused,

and just enough freedom to find their own limits—and break through them.

If we could build that?

That would change everything.

Because when people are trusted to stretch, they rise.

And once they do,

they never go back.

We built the system.

Now it was time to test it.

We opened the doors with thirteen students and one of the best teachers there was—Nelson Brown, who's now our Dean of Education.

Nelson wasn't just thrown into a classroom. He was thrown into the build. Before he could teach, he had to experience it. I paired him with two of our best construction guys and said, "Build the unit."

And not just any unit—the first unit. A kitchen module. That same module he built still sits on our property today, a reminder that we all started as learners. And that if you build the right environment, it will teach you.

Nelson had a master's in education. He had taught at an institute. But this? This was different. This wasn't theoretical. This was hands-on. And as he worked, he started asking questions—good ones. Questions about how this model would scale. How it would adapt. How we would handle X or Y when it came up.

My answer?

"I don't know. Hypothetically, this should happen . . . but there's no book for this. We'll find out when we get there."

He asked again later.

Same answer.

We were all discovering this as we went. Nelson just happened to be the first to walk through the fire and take notes.

We built the system.

Now it was time to test it.

So we opened the doors—no fanfare, no ribbon cutting.

Just one scratched-up table, one big idea . . .

and thirteen students crazy enough to bet their future on something that didn't exist six months earlier.

Over the next six months, those thirteen students built fifteen homes, one unit at a time.

They started with a simple office module—no plumbing, just basic framing and electrical.

It was designed for one reason: to build confidence.

And it worked.

From there, they built modules that connected into full one-bed, one-bath homes. One by one, 199 square feet at a time, they leveled up.

No lectures. No busywork. Just the build.

And the environment did the teaching.

There were communication breakdowns.

Frustration.

Heat.

Sawdust.

Mistakes.

Arguments.

Moments that almost broke them.

But also—breakthroughs.

They started catching mistakes before they happened.

They started stepping in without being told.

They started trusting their instincts—and each other.

They stopped asking, *Can I do this?*

And started saying, *I've got it.*

And then one day, they stood back and looked at what they had built.

Not just a frame.

Not just a floor.

A house.

A real house. Something solid. Tangible. The kind of thing most people never believe they could create with their own two hands.

And something in them shifted.

Because when you build a house—

something in *you* gets built too.

Confidence.

Capability.

Grit.

The kind that doesn't wash off with sawdust or fade when the job is done.

It stays.

Because now, they didn't just *think* they were builders.

They *knew.*

One of those thirteen was Kasandra Prieto.

She wasn't your typical trade school student. Kasandra was already a powerhouse—smart, successful, and thriving as a real estate agent. She didn't need a second career. She didn't need a fallback plan. She came because she wanted more—more depth, more hands-on knowledge, more confidence in what she was selling. And what happened inside that build? It changed her.

She went from sharp to unstoppable.

At first, she was like a lot of our students—unsure how to use a power tool, second-guessing her cuts, nervous about getting it wrong. But by the end, she was calling shots, coaching teammates, and stepping into leadership like she'd been doing it for years. The house she built was impressive. But the person she became? That was the real transformation.

And here's the kicker: She didn't just graduate and move on. Kasandra took what she learned and wove it back into her business. She became a more authentic advisor to her clients—because now, when she talked about construction, she didn't have to pretend. She'd lived it.

Today, she's not only a top-tier professional—she's a force for good. One of the most talented marketers I've ever seen. The kind of person who doesn't just talk about believing in something—she shows up, she builds it, and then she tells the world.

Kasandra isn't just a success story. She's a blueprint for what happens when you take a strong, capable woman and put her in an environment that recognizes her potential—and then hands her a hammer. She already had the fire. We just gave her the space to prove it, and she lit the whole place up.

And she wasn't the only one.

That first class sparked something we couldn't contain.

Then Came the Momentum

We had proven the model.

And the word got out.

Within four months, we'd quadrupled in size.

Sixty students enrolled in the next class.

We moved into a new facility just to keep up with demand.

We were ready.

But what we didn't know was this:

The government wasn't going to let that kind of momentum go unchecked.

They didn't celebrate what we'd done.

They didn't care that students were learning, lives were changing, or that we were filling a massive workforce gap.

They didn't try to understand us.

They tried to contain us. And so—like any bloated bureaucracy caught off guard—they did what they do best:

They weaponized regulation.

The AZDOH Mess

At one point, we were told the Arizona Department of Housing wouldn't even inspect our facility—because it was in Tucson, and they were "no longer traveling to Tucson."

Seriously.

Their solution?

"Here's a list of third-party inspectors."

A three-page list.

Not a single one was located in Arizona.

Not one would come to Tucson.

I ended up convincing a company in Florida to hire someone in Tucson just to do the inspection.

And the moment I locked that in?

"Actually, never mind. We'll come to Tucson now."

And when they did?

They didn't give us a report—which, by law, they were required to do.

Second inspection? Same thing.

When I raised hell with the assistant director, they finally sent us the second report.

A week later, they backdated and sent the first.

It would be funny if it weren't so ridiculous.

Meanwhile, our students had already built forty modular units— real homes, not hypotheticals.

We had one and a half million dollars in finished inventory lined up like trophies on the lot, and over six million dollars in signed pre- sales ready to roll.

And the state's big response?

"You can't place those units on Arizona soil."

Didn't matter that they were already sold.

Didn't matter that students poured their blood, their sweat, and forty hours a week into building them.

Didn't matter that we checked every box—except the one they for- got to mention until six months later.

We were ready to deliver homes. They wanted more paperwork.

It was like winning the race and getting disqualified because your shoes weren't preapproved by a committee that doesn't run.

We didn't get shut down because we failed.

We got shut down because we moved faster than the fax machine in their office could handle.

And yeah, we were hurting.

The cash flow dried up faster than an Arizona riverbed in July.

We weren't just stuck—we were stuck with a parking lot full of houses and a government that couldn't decide if we were a school, a manufacturer, or a threat to their filing system.

Enter the Neeleman Brothers

Then the clouds parted—kind of.

My business partner had the idea to reach out to Steve Neeleman—yes, *those* Neelemans.

One founded **JetBlue.**

Another started **HealthEquity.**

We weren't pitching a product. We were asking for a little investment, maybe even some guidance. But when they saw what we were doing, they didn't offer advice.

They made an offer.

"We'll take your units at our resort, Zion Ponderosa Ranch in Utah."

And not just any units—these were the very homes our students had built. The ones we couldn't place in Arizona. The ones sitting on our lot, fully finished, fully inspected, and completely banned from use in the state they were built in.

The Neelemans didn't just see potential—they saw a real solution.

High-quality housing. Fast turnaround. Affordable builds. All in a region that didn't have a massive labor force to pull from.

Just like that, the mission had a pulse again.

- We got licensed in Utah.

- Got inspected.

- I got my contractor's license.

- And we moved forty units five hundred miles through the snow.

- Then installed them—legally—during the biggest snowstorm in Utah history.

All before Arizona could approve a single permit.

Let that sink in.

We built the homes.

Reinspected them.

Drove them across state lines.

Got approved.

Installed them.

Before our home state could figure out how to label us.

Infuriating? Yes.

Validating? Also yes.

AZDOH is still playing the same games to this day.

Still dragging their feet.

Still changing the rules mid-process.

Still acting like innovation is a threat instead of a solution.

Round Two: Postsecondary Education

But we weren't done getting sucker punched.

Right as we were catching our breath, the Arizona Department of Postsecondary Education called.

"You're not exempt under our standards. You're operating illegally."

Boom. Shut down again.

This time they made us cancel our entire class of sixty students.

Staff hired.

Curriculum built.

Everything ready to go—scrapped.

But here's the twist:

This department actually worked with us.

They were fast. Professional. Clear.

They helped us get licensed within two months.

Still a blow, but this time we could recover faster.

Fighting to Stay Alive

What didn't stop—no matter how hard they tried—were the sales.

We got creative.

We got scrappy.

And we started selling homes, selling units, selling solutions—anywhere we could.

Some deals were small, some were big. Some came through relationships we'd been building for years. Others? Total surprises.

One of the most powerful shifts?

We started selling to Native American reservations.

These were communities that understood the value of the product, the need for housing, and the urgency to get things done. They didn't need to be sold on innovation—they needed solutions. And they saw what we were doing for what it was: real.

Every sale bought us time.

Every delivery proved we were still moving.

Every customer became a believer—and a megaphone.

And every time we made a sale, we got stronger.

Every time we delivered, we gained ground.

That's what kept us going.

Not handouts—sales.

Because we weren't asking for permission.

We were solving real problems.

And the market knew it—even if the state didn't.

Chapter 28

Where We Go from Here: The Turning Point

We didn't come this far just to build houses.

Yes, construction was our battleground. It's where we proved the model worked. It's where the vision got forged in sweat, sawdust, and late-night prayers. But this—this whole Idea'l thing?

It was never just about construction.

Construction was the test case. The lab. The training ground.

But the system we've built? It goes way beyond trades.

We accidentally stumbled into a universal law of learning:

If you create the right environment, it will teach.

And when people are immersed in that environment, they learn faster, retain more, and come out transformed—not just trained.

That's the secret we unlocked.

And now that we know it works?

We're not stopping at framing and roofing.

And here's where it gets real—for you, the reader.

Because whether you want to build a business, launch a movement, develop a team, or just grow into the version of yourself you know you're meant to be . . .

You've got to build the environment first.

If you want to become something great, immerse yourself in it.

Don't just study the theory—step into the space where growth happens.

You don't learn how to lead by reading about leadership.

You lead. You get it wrong. You adjust. You keep going.

You don't build confidence by dreaming—you build it by doing.

Want to be an entrepreneur?

Get around entrepreneurs. Start selling something. Feel the risk.

Want to change an industry?

Start inside the problem and work your way out.

Want to lead a team?

Build an environment that brings the best out of people—and be the first to go all in.

Because the fastest way to become something . . . is to *do* it.

And the fastest way to do it well . . . is to *build the environment that teaches you along the way.*

That's what we learned.

That's what Idea'l is.

And that's where everything changes.

Education Reimagined

The future of education isn't more lectures.

It's not longer degrees, shinier certificates, or better flashcards.

It's not about fancier classrooms or the latest overpriced tech.

It's about one thing: environments that actually work.

Idea'l proved something most people still don't understand:

When you stop talking *about* learning and start *doing* the thing—you don't just create smarter students.

You create different people.

People who believe in themselves.

People who've felt what it means to build, to lead, to solve, to screw up, and get back up.

People who walk differently because they know, deep down:

"I can do this."

And here's the wild part:

This model doesn't belong to construction.

We just happened to start there.

It works in tech.

It works in healthcare.

It works in agriculture, manufacturing, aviation, robotics—

Probably even works in underwater basket weaving if you let the environment do the teaching.

Because once you understand the secret sauce—

once you realize that **experience is the education**—

everything changes.

You stop chasing information, and you start chasing *transformation*.

You stop waiting for the "right moment." You stop trying to learn your way into confidence.

Instead, you get in the game.

You don't build confidence from a screen.

You don't find purpose through scrolls and algorithms.

And you definitely don't learn grit from a YouTube tutorial.

You learn it by doing the thing.

By showing up.

By taking risks.

By failing in real time—and learning to keep going.

If you want to start a business—*start*.

If you want to lead—*lead*.

If you want to build something that lasts—*build it now, while it still scares you.*

And if you want a family?

Get married. Have kids.

You'll never be financially "ready." You'll never feel perfectly prepared.

But that's the point.

The greatest things in life don't wait for your budget to catch up.

They show up when your heart is ready—even if your spreadsheet isn't.

That's the secret nobody tells you:

You don't get ready for life by watching it.

You get ready for life by *living* it.

Talk to people. Try the thing. Launch the idea. Love the person. Build the dream.

And when it breaks?

Good. Now you've got something to rebuild stronger.

Every great story starts with a moment when someone said,

"I'm not ready—but I'm going anyway."

So go.

Let the experience teach you.

Let the challenge shape you.

Let failure stretch you.

Let the work change you.

Because *you won't learn who you are until you get out there and start becoming it.*

That's the foundation we're building on.

Not lectures.

Not theory.

But lived-in, hands-on, real-world learning that transforms people from the inside out.

We're not fixing school.

We're building something that finally works.

Humans 2.0 (with Upgraded Wiring)

We've seen it firsthand:

- A real estate agent becomes a confident crew lead.

- A train engineer trades steel rails for steel frames—and thrives.

- Young adults with zero experience start building homes like they've done it for years.

This isn't a theory anymore. It's a pattern.
Drop people into a high-intensity, real-world environment—
and watch them transform.
Not slowly. Not academically.
But through sweat, pressure, and moments that *actually matter*.
This isn't just education reform.
It's a reintroduction to what humans are capable of.
We were made to build.
To problem-solve.
To rise to a challenge and become stronger on the other side.
We've just spent the last few decades training that instinct out of people.
But here's the truth:
When you put a human in the right environment—
they don't just learn faster.
They wake up.
The spark returns. The confidence builds. The excuses die.
And what's left is someone who finally remembers what they're made of.
That's what we're after.
Not better test scores.
Better people.
People who are calm in chaos.

People who can lead under pressure.

People who take ownership, solve problems, and follow through.

That's what the world is starving for.

Not more degrees. More *doers*.

And if this is what we've unlocked in one industry—

just imagine what happens when it spreads.

And here's the thing—

You're not reading this by accident.

It's because *something in you* knows you were made for more.

You've lived through things that should've taken you out—but didn't.

You've carried weight that others couldn't see—and you kept showing up anyway.

You may not feel like a leader.

But you are.

A leader in your home.

A leader in your work.

A leader in your circle, your crew, your corner of the world.

Your experiences—the wins, the losses, the stuff no one clapped for?

That's your training. That's your credibility. That's your *edge*.

You don't have to be the loudest voice in the room to lead.

You just have to be the one willing to step forward.

So if you're looking around and thinking,

This system doesn't work.

Or

There's got to be a better way.

Good news.

That means *you're the one* who's supposed to build it.

We're Not Done Yet

If you've made it this far, I want you to hear this loud and clear:

This story wasn't about construction.

It wasn't about real estate.

It wasn't even about education.

It was about what happens when someone refuses to quit.

It was about a kid from Tucson with no pedigree, no trust fund, and no clue what he was doing—just enough conviction to figure it out anyway.

And now?

Now it's about **you.**

Because this world doesn't need more spectators.

It needs more people willing to **build what doesn't exist yet.**

You've lived through things that have shaped you.

You've overcome things you don't talk about.

And whether you know it or not, those moments gave you something rare:

Perspective. Vision. Fire.

So what do you do with that?

You **start.**

I did.

I kept asking, trying, getting back up, praying, listening, showing up—even when I was broke, confused, or totally in over my head.

And over time—slowly, painfully, and with more face-plants than I can count—God started handing me the blueprint.

Not in one big reveal.

Not in lightning bolts or burning bushes.

But little by little—just slow enough that I could actually understand it when I got there.

I tried to rush it.

He was always trying to show me a better way.

And yeah, I ignored Him more than once.

But He stayed with me—patient, persistent, and just quiet enough that I had to get still and really listen.

That's how this all came together.

Not from brilliance.

Not from luck.

But from grit, grace, and one hard-earned lesson at a time.

So hear me when I say this:

This story?

This book?

It's not about me.

It's about what happens when someone finally decides,

"I'm gonna build what doesn't exist yet."

If you've got that nudge—that fire—that itch in your soul that won't shut up, that thing you can't unsee . . .

Then you're probably the one who's supposed to do it.

Not when you have all the answers.

Not when the timing is perfect.

Not when the money shows up.

Now.

Start messy.

Start scared.

Start underqualified.

But start.

The world doesn't need more people waiting in line.

It needs more builders.

More risk-takers.

More people crazy enough to say,

"You know what? I'll go first."

So stop waiting for permission.

Because if no one else is going to do it?

Maybe that's because it's supposed to be you.

And when you're ready to build—when you're ready to stop talking and start swinging?

We'll be here.

Still showing up.

Still solving.

Still building the future.

You're not alone. And neither are we.

There are thousands of us out there—builders, dreamers, fighters—cheering for you.

We want you to win. We need you to win.

And when you do?

We'll be here to celebrate with you.

Let's go.

One More Flight

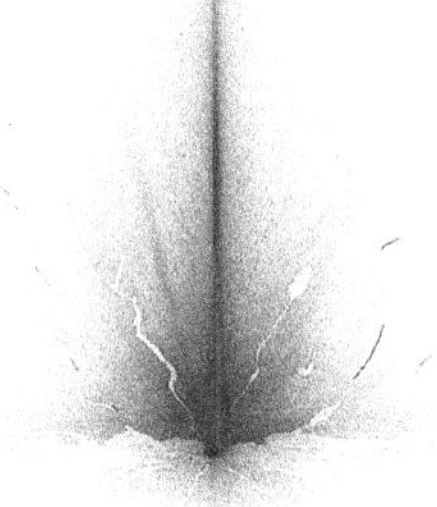

By now, you've seen the parallels.

This book wasn't about hang gliding.

It wasn't about Cutco.

Or clowns.

Or dance.

It wasn't about heartbreak, real estate, school licenses, or modular housing.

It was about flying.

Because that's what this whole thing has been—a story of what it means to fly.

To run toward something with everything you've got.

To fail, crash, laugh, try again.

To be scared out of your mind and do it anyway.

To rise higher than you ever thought you could—and fall harder than you ever wanted to.

To chase something invisible, something wild and free, something bigger than yourself . . . and catch just enough of it to keep going.

You've been with me through every phase of that journey.

From boinking the ground with clown shoes and balloon animals.

To learning to sell knives with a duffel bag and way too much optimism.

To chasing love, chasing meaning, chasing purpose across borders, breakups, and bold ideas.

To flipping houses, building schools, and licensing programs I didn't even know how to spell when I started.

To falling flat, praying harder, and refusing to quit.

All of it was just learning to fly.

And like Eric taught us on that hill in Sonoita, there are four things that matter if you want to stay in the air:

- Eyes—Lock on to the vision. Don't pretend the obstacles aren't there—but don't stare at them, either. Focus on where you're going, not what you're afraid of.

- Hands—Grip when you need control. Let go when it's time to trust. If you're still micromanaging everything, you're fighting the very thing you built.

- Body Position—Posture under pressure. How you carry yourself affects everyone around you. Lean in when it's time to lead. Stay balanced when things start to sway.

- Run Like Hell—When the moment comes, go. Not halfway. Not kinda-sorta. All in. Sprint. Launch. Trust the wing.

And then there's the **Thermal Rule:**
You can only rise with the thermals you find—or create.
Some will come to you.
Some you'll have to go find.
Some will be disguised as failure.
But when you find one—ride it for all it's worth.
And always know where you'll land if it disappears.

You don't need to be perfect to fly.

You just need to commit.

To run with your whole heart.

To lead with your whole soul.

To love what you're building enough to risk the fall.

That's how you lead.

That's how you grow.

That's how you fly.

But let's be clear: This book?

This wasn't the mountaintop. This was the bunny hill.

This was the run-up.

The messy takeoff.

The scared-kid-with-a-dream phase.

And if you've made it this far with me, you've got wings of your own now.

You've seen what's possible.

You've learned how to run.

And you've got the scars to prove it.

So here's what I want you to remember:

Keep your eyes locked on the goal, even when everything around you is screaming for attention. Know when to grip and when to glide. Hold your posture when everything shakes. And when the opportunity comes—when it's time to go—run like hell.

Because the world needs more builders. More leaders.

More people who run toward the edge instead of backing away.

More people who know how to fly.

Now go. Your next thermal is out there. And when you catch it?

Soar.

Acknowledgments

To God, first—because none of this exists without Him. Every breakthrough, every breath, every miracle along the way was His doing, not mine.

To Candice, my wife and the love of my life. Thank you for believing in me, forgiving me, supporting me, challenging me, and walking with me through every chapter—especially the ones no one sees.

To my children, Lyza, Lily, Jesse, Rose, and Dacey, you inspire me to build a world worthy of your future.

To my parents, for doing the best they could and giving me a foundation to grow from.

To my brother Scott, whose journey reshaped my heart and clarified my mission. This book doesn't exist without you.

And to my brothers and sisters — thank you for growing up with me, for shaping me in ways you may never fully see.

To the friends, mentors, students, teachers, investors, partners, supporters, prayer warriors, and every person who showed up at the exact moment I needed them—thank you. Your fingerprints are on every page.

To Shane, my brother in the sky. You changed my life, and your legacy lives on in these words.

And finally, to every underdog, late starter, misfit, dropout, restless soul, and hands-on learner who was told they weren't enough. This book is for you.

Notes

1. Reuell, Peter. "Study shows students in 'active learning' classrooms learn more than they think." *The Harvard Gazette.* September 4, 2019. https://news.harvard.edu/gazette/story/2019/09/study -shows-that-students-learn-more-when-taking-part-in-classrooms -that-employ-active-learning-strategies/

2. Chan, et al. "Effects of Experiential Learning Programmes on Adolescent Prosocial Behavior, Empathy, and Subjective Well-being: A Systematic Review and Meta-Analysis." August 4, 2021. *Frontiers in Psychology.* https://doi.org/10.3389/fpsyg.2021.709699

3. Sahito, Z. H., Khoso, F. J., & Phulpoto, J. "The Effectiveness of Active Learning Strategies in Enhancing Student Engagement and Academic Performance." January 2025. *Journal of Social Sciences Review,* 5(1), 110–127, https://doi.org/10.62843/jssr.v5i1.471

4. Paivio, Allan. *Mind and Its Evolution: A Dual Coding Theoretical Approach,* 1st Edition. Psychology Press, 2014.

5. Mayer, Richard E., and Roxana Moreno. "Nine Ways to Reduce Cognitive Load in Multimedia Learning." 2003. *Educational Psychologist,* 38(1): 43–52. https://doi.org/10.1207/S15326985EP3801_6

6. Shams, et al. "Influences of Multisensory Experience on Subsequent Unisensory Processing." October 18, 2011. *Frontiers in Psychology.* https://doi.org/10.3389/fpsyg.2011.00264

7. Dwyer, Francis. *Strategies for Improving Visual Learning: A Handbook for the Effective Selection, Design, and Use of Visualized Materials.* The University of Michigan: Learning Services, 1978.

8. Oswald, Daniel F., and Michael Molenda. "A Conversation with Michael Molenda." 2003. *Educational Technology,* 43(2): 59–63. http://www.jstor.org/stable/44428826

9. Gibson, Eleanor. *Principles of Perceptual Learning and Development.* Pearson College, 1969.

To the Reader

Thank you for reading this book. If these pages encouraged you, pushed you, challenged you, or lit something inside you, I'd love to hear from you. And if you feel led, leaving a review is one of the best ways to help this message reach more people who need it.

Your story matters. Your work matters. And the world needs what you're building. Keep going.

—Clay

If this book helped you in any way, would you take thirty seconds to leave a review?

Your review helps this book reach the people who were never meant to sit still, the ones who feel left behind, and the ones who are ready to build something that lasts. You can also stay connected and follow future projects, books, and ideas at abernathypublishing.com. Thank you for being part of this journey.